Evaluating Health Program
Impact

Evaluating Health Program Impact

The U.S.-Yugoslav
Cooperative Research Effort

Ralph E. Berry, Jr.
Harvard University School of
    Public Health

with

Mark G. Field
Boston University

John A. Karefa-Smart
Harvard University

Dieter Koch-Weser
Harvard University

Mark S. Thompson
Institute for Applied Systems
    Analysis, Laxenburg, Austria

Lexington Books
D.C. Heath and Company
Lexington, Massachusetts
Toronto   London

Library of Congress Cataloging in Publication Data
Main entry under title:

Evaluating health program impact.

   1. Public health research—Evaluation. 2. Public health research—Yugoslavia. 3. Economic assistance, American—Yugoslavia. I. Berry, Ralph E.
[DNLM: 1. Evaluation studies. 2. International cooperation. 3. Research
support—Yugoslavia. WA20.5 E92]

RA440.6.E93   362.1'07'20497   74-9921
ISBN 0-669-94771-7

Published simultaneously in Canada.

Printed in the United States of America.

International Standard Book Number: 0-669-94771-7

Library of Congress Catalog Card Number: 74-9921

Contents

List of Tables

Foreword

Although "program evaluation" by the federal government has received a great deal of publicity, formal activities in this direction, by most agencies, are still very much in their infancy. Evaluation of major federal health programs, as a distinguishable function, was legislatively recognized only in 1970, with the enactment of Section 513 of the Public Health Service Act. Section 513 authorized the secretary of the Department of Health, Education, and Welfare to set aside "not more than 1 per centum of any appropriation . . . under any provision of this Act . . . for evaluation (directly, or by grants or contracts) of any program authorized by this Act."

The Department of Health, Education, and Welfare's health evaluation program is still very much in its gestation period. Its Division of Health Evaluation, set up to implement Section 513, has in effect functioned more as a laboratory in program evaluation than as an established unit, aware of a well-defined mandate and a set of clearly delineated activities. The first three years of its existence have been largely ones of testing and probing, of attempting to define its *own* functions as well as those of the evaluation activity itself.

As one of its first analyses, the Division of Health Evaluation commissioned Harvard University to perform "An Evaluation Study of the Special Foreign Currency Program in Yugoslavia." Taken by itself, this study was a vital one, irrespective of its locus and origins. P.L. 480 monies ("excess currencies") were, by June 1971, quickly becoming a scarce national resource. Discussions were imminent on the future direction of the program. Yet hard data on the impact of the program during its first seventeen years were largely unavailable. Thus, the study, even taken solely as a discrete piece of analysis, was to prove valuable.

This study assumed an even more important role when seen in the broader perspective of the Division's attempt to specify the nature of the health evaluation function as a whole. As one of the first analytic activities launched by the Division, the study, both initially and during its entire tenure, paralleled simultaneous Division attempts to formulate its own approach to the evaluative function. At a very practical level, the study graphically reflects those attempts. Its conduct was largely dependent on the resolution of a number of very basic issues regarding program evaluation: What is the ultimate purpose of evaluation? How does one determine an evaluation staff's analytic focus? Which issues deserve attention and which can safely be ignored? Which types of analytic tools are best applied to policy analysis? Do they differ from those employed in more traditional research activities?

As much as any study initiated by the Division of Health Evaluation, the evaluation of the Special Foreign Currency Program forced both the contractor and the Division staff to address and resolve many such issues. The document at hand is, I think, indicative of the fact that most of those issues were successfully identified and met.

Perhaps the most significant part of the study is the degree to which the study sensitized all participants to the ultimate purpose of evaluation, namely, to serve the "needs of the decision maker." If we assume that the central core of the managerial and political function is the making of policies and of decisions to implement these policies, then evaluation can be seen as the basic strategic tool in the performance of this function. As the authors have indicated, "evaluation involves marshaling information that will serve the purpose of improving decisions." Only from within the perspective of a prior assessment of the needs of the decision-maker can the program evaluator adequately address the issues enumerated above. It is the decision-making process that must stipulate the focus and methods of program evaluation. The success of evaluation will be measured by the degree to which it furnishes data relevant at the actual point of decision.

Had it accomplished nothing more than focusing the attention of one federal evaluation staff on that very simple truth, this study would have far exceeded in value the resources devoted to it.

Paul R. Willging, Ph.D., Director
Division of Health Evaluation
Office of the Secretary
Department of Health, Education,
  and Welfare

Preface

In May 1971, the Department of Health, Education, and Welfare requested proposals to conduct an evaluative study of the impact of the Special Foreign Currency Program in Yugoslavia administered by the Office of International Health. The study, sponsored by the Division of Health Evaluation of the Department of Health, Education, and Welfare, was intended to evaluate the impact of the program on both the United States and Yugoslavia. In fact, two separate but integrated evaluations were undertaken. An assessment of the impact of the program on the United States was primarily the responsibility of an evaluation team at Harvard University. An assessment of the impact of the program on Yugoslavia was primarily the responsibility of an evaluation team in Yugoslavia.

The authors were members of the evaluation team at Harvard, and this book is based essentially on the evaluative efforts of the Harvard team. The study was designed as an evaluation of an existing specific program, and as such is clearly most relevant to that program. In large part, however, this book was written because it seems quite likely that the experience gained, the techniques employed, and the insights provided can contribute to other programs as well.

The evaluation study involved significant efforts on the part of many, and the authors owe a debt of gratitude to all. Foremost, of course, there were the other members of the evaluation team. Alexander Langmuir, Edward Murray, Jerome Peterson, and John Thompson were involved in the extensive review of the more than one hundred projects that comprised the Special Foreign Currency Program in Yugoslavia. In fact, the overall study was a team effort. Further, there were several members of the staff of the project who made significant contributions to the overall study and who in many respects were part of the team effort. James Barkas and Tatiana Barkas provided continuous and consistent support in the form of background research and data analysis. Vicki George served the project as an executive secretary—which the team came to learn meant that she was responsible for what seemed at times an infinite set of tasks.

Three individuals came to serve the needs of the project at particularly crucial times. Nicole Urban was responsible for much of the computer analysis as it appears. Mary Louise Fisher labored long and well over several drafts of the report and the manuscript. Finally, Dorothy Berry served the senior author well above and beyond the normal call of duty, and at one point served the project much as a human computer.

The efforts of the Yugoslav evaluation team were critical. In fact, the two teams coordinated their activities to mutual advantage. A number of joint meetings among several members of each team contributed to the overall effort, and the authors are clearly indebted to and appreciative of the Yugoslav evaluation team. (The members of the Yugoslav team are listed on p. 145.)

Finally, the project could not have been completed without the support and assistance of many members of the Department of Health, Education, and Welfare. Paul Willging was the Project Officer representing the Division of Health Evaluation and his efforts in that role made our task the easier. Linda Vogel, of the Office of International Health, was of invaluable aid to the project throughout its entire tenure, consistently providing support and assistance. In addition, many staff members of the several agencies took the time from busy schedules to assist our team by providing information, data, and insights without which our efforts would surely have been the more difficult, if not impossible.

1 Introduction

The Special Foreign Currency Program is an international health research program financed out of U.S.-owned foreign currency in excess of requirements as determined by the Treasury Department. The program, which has been in operation for thirteen years, presently is administered by the Office of International Health and involves the National Institutes of Health, Health Services and Mental Health Administration, and the Food and Drug Administration among the agencies of the Department of Health, Education, and Welfare. Over the years twelve countries have participated in the program.

Although the international health research program has grown in size and scope since its inception in fiscal 1961, the program is quite small relative to the yearly operating budgets of the participating agencies. Nevertheless, the program can provide a valuable alternative resource for the achievement of domestic health objectives. Given the constraints upon the availability of dollars for the support of scientific activities, both in the United States and abroad, the utilization of excess foreign currencies is a valuable resource. Since a variety of important and unique research opportunities of potential usefulness exists in excess-currency countries, the Special Foreign Currency Program is capable of developing knowledge and insights that might not otherwise be forthcoming.

In May 1971, the Department of Health, Education, and Welfare requested proposals to conduct an evaluative study of the impact of the Special Foreign Currency Program in Yugoslavia administered by the Office of International Health. The study was intended to evaluate the impact of the program on both the United States and Yugoslavia. The study was sponsored by the Division of Health Evaluation of the Department of Health, Education, and Welfare.

In general terms, according to the original request for proposals, the study was intended to assess the impact of the Special Foreign Currency Program in both countries in order to bring about an improved program in the future. The study was designed, in fact, to involve two separate though integrated evaluation projects, and two contracts were awarded. An assessment of the impact of the program on the United States was primarily to be the responsibility of an evaluation team at Harvard University. The assessment of the impact of the program on Yugoslavia was primarily to be the responsibility of an evaluation team in Yugoslavia.

The two teams did in fact coordinate their activities to mutual advantage. The basic strategies of evaluation and criteria for evaluation employed by the two teams were similar. A number of joint meetings were held involving several members of each team. Most important, the efforts of the two teams were mutually reenforcing. Since they were performing under separate contracts, each team generated a separate report. The purpose of this book is to outline in some detail the principal results of the evaluative efforts of the Harvard team.

Although the study was commissioned for very practical reasons, such as assessing the impact of the program and improving its administration, it is hoped that its value is broader than the specific area to which it addressed itself. It may therefore contribute to the general literature on program and policy evaluation, and be of help to those in the government, in private agencies, and in industry who are concerned about the value of what they do, whether what they do "makes a difference" or not, what kind of a difference, and the degree to which their plans and goals have been realized through the deliberate and consious process of purposive action, policy, and programming.

Evaluation in Principle

Even a brief and relatively superficial survey of literature dealing with the topic of evaluation uncovers a breadth of concept covered by the term. In fact, the working definition of the concept as applied by those engaged in this evaluation project has been modified over the actual period of the study. This modification is viewed as appropriate and the resultant report should consequently prove the more useful to decision-makers in the Department of Health, Education, and Welfare.

As the study progressed, the participants came to an appreciation that any evaluation, if it is to have its maximum potential effectiveness, must serve the needs of the decision-maker. This report is based on a simple, straightforward, and useful interpretation of evaluation—evaluation involves marshaling information that will serve the purpose of improving decisions.

The Form of the Study

The study commissioned by the Division of Health Evaluation was intended to assess the impact of the Special Foreign Currency Program on both the United States and Yugoslavia. The contract with Harvard University specified two primary goals for the study:

1. To assess the contribution of the program for the achievement of the domestic health goals of the United States, particularly those defined by HEW's health agencies; and

2. To evaluate and measure the substantive results and the impact of the program on the host country, i.e., Yugoslavia.

Simultaneous achievement of these goals involved the parallel efforts of the Harvard team and the Yugoslav team.

In order to complete the study with any degree of success, it was necessary to:

1. Delineate the domestic health objectives of both countries;

2. Devise a methodology and technique for assessing impact; and

3. Ascertain the kinds of information that would be most useful to decision-makers.

These requirements dictated the broad form of the study.

The major efforts of both teams were brought to bear on each of these areas in turn. The tasks were not trivial, and many problems were encountered that affected the final evaluation. On balance, however, it is felt that the overall evaluation was reasonably successful and should be of considerable usefulness to the relevant decision-makers.

An Outline of the Study Report

An historical overview of the Special Foreign Currency Program is outlined in Chapter 2. This overview was originally proposed to provide the Harvard evaluation team members with the necessary and appropriate background information for their specific efforts. It should serve to focus the relevant perspective of this report. Since a primary objective of the general program is to contribute to the domestic health objectives of the United States, an explanation of the derivation of the list of these objectives is also included in Chapter 2.

An overview of the Special Foreign Currency Program in Yugoslavia is outlined in Chapter 3. This overview benefits not only from the project data available, but also from the separate perspectives of the Harvard team and the Yugoslav team.

The primary technique for gathering data relevant to the impact of projects involved a standard questionnaire for project review. Since each project was reviewed at least twice by the Harvard team and at least once by the Yugoslav team, a variety of information was available for analysis. Administrative information, information concerning relative progress, cooperative efforts, project impact, and other data have been analyzed and the results are outlined in some detail in Chapter 4. In essence, the analysis of the project reviews is used as a basis for a general discussion of the impact of the program.

Since the decision-maker is concerned not only with what has happened but also with any information that might contribute to improvements in the program in the future, an attempt was made to gain insight into how the impact may or may not be affected by the administration of the program. Thus,

Chapter 4 includes suggestions for improving the impact of the program by making certain administrative adjustments.

Also included in Chapter 4 is a separate analysis of projects characterized by significant cost overruns. Finally, there is a general discussion of the feasibility of identifying guidelines for distinguishing between projects with high and low expected impacts.

There are a number of quite different types of projects. In order to gain insight a number of special in-depth analyses were done for certain program types. Chapter 5 includes an outline of the results of special analyses of student exchange programs, conferences, translations, and critical reviews of literature.

Chapter 6 includes a summary of the major findings of the evaluation study, and a series of recommendations.

Some Problems

A number of problems were encountered in the process of this study. There were problems of a substantive, of an administrative, and of a logistical nature. In assessing this report, these problems, whether anticipated or unanticipated, should be kept in mind. This is especially relevant to the extent that several of the problems may have had a direct effect on the results as reported.

Most of the problems encountered and their effect on the effort are described in some detail where appropriate in each of the chapters that follow. It should suffice for introductory purposes to simply outline some of these problems.

The issue of impact was a primary substantive concern from the outset. What is impact? How is impact to be measured? This concern was present for both evaluation teams throughout the study. The result of grappling with this problem over time was a working definition that could claim the support of some consensus at least of a rough order of magnitude. It should be obvious that the result was not an objective measurement, but rather a subjective assessment. The strength of the assessment presumably derives in part from the experience of the reviewers, but in the main, from the averaging of multiple opinions.

One problem that is more thorny than assessing actual impact is assessing potential impact. At the very least it is more complicated by the requirement that subjective probabilities of success need also to be assessed. It was apparently thought that the age of the program—eleven years—would make possible an actual impact orientation of the evaluation. The Special Foreign Currency Program in Yugoslavia is in fact overwhelmingly a recent program. This dimension of the program is quite evident in the summary of project starting and ending dates outlined in Tables 1-1 and 1-2. Of the 110 projects evaluated, 51 had not started by the first of 1971. More significant, 95 of the projects were not scheduled to be completed by the end of 1971. Only 9 projects began operations during the first six years of the program. Of the 15 projects scheduled

Table 1-1

Summary of Project Starting Dates of the Special Foreign Currency Program in Yugoslavia

Project Starting Date	Number of Projects by Agency				
	NIH	HSMHA	FDA	EPA	Total
1960	1	–	–	–	1
1961	–	–	–	–	–
1962	1	–	–	–	1
1963	–	1	–	–	1
1964	–	3	–	–	3
1965	–	3	–	–	3
1966	2	1	–	–	3
1967	–	7	–	–	7
1968	3	12	–	–	15
1969	2	13	2	–	17
1970	3	3	1	1	8
1971	20	25	4	–	49
1972	–	2	–	–	2
Total	32	70	7	1	110

Table 1-2

Summary of Project Ending Dates of the Special Foreign Currency Program in Yugoslavia

Project Ending Date	Number of Projects by Agency				
	NIH	HSMHA	FDA	EPA	Total
1966	–	1	–	–	1
1967	–	–	–	–	–
1968	–	1	–	–	1
1969	–	1	–	–	1
1970	–	3	–	1	4
1971	2	6	–	–	8
1972	4	12	–	–	16
1973	5	17	3	–	25
1974	21	5	3	–	29
1975	–	9	1	–	10
1976	–	11	–	–	11
1977	–	4	–	–	4
Total	32	70	7	1	110

to end by 1971, most were so recent that they had not yet attained publication, while other publications probably had not had the time to achieve near full impact. Thus, in the vast majority of cases the evaluation teams had to make projections of potential impact rather than attempt to measure actual impact. The nature of the program is such that this problem is more pronounced for assessing impact in the United States than in Yugoslavia, but only slightly so.

Given that the program is in fact such a recent one in terms of relative magnitudes, the implications for this evaluation study are somewhat mixed. On the one hand, it could be argued that the evaluation study was perhaps premature. Certainly in terms of assessing actual impact it must be judged premature. On the other hand, since evaluation should be designed to marshal information that will serve the purpose of improving decisions, the fact that a major proportion of program activity presumably is subject to future decisions augurs well for an earlier evaluation. The issue should be judged by the relevant decision-makers after they have analyzed the report, but the problem should be kept in mind as the report is read.

The basic data source for most of the analysis of this report was the standard questionnaire for project review. Inconsistent interpretation of questions was recognized as a potential problem early in the process. Although every effort was made to insure a consistency of interpretation of questions among the several reviewers, there is some evidence that complete success cannot be claimed in this regard.

Paucity of information in certain cases did pose a problem in assessing impact. The reviewers on the Harvard team had to rely primarily on project files provided by the Office of International Health. The informational value of these files varied greatly for a number of obvious reasons. Some files were quite sufficient, others were characterized by a paucity of information. In many instances, additional information was available by the simple mechanism of a telephone conversation with the project officer.

The Yugoslav team also examined all available documents. Less information was available in the project files in Yugoslavia, but they did have the compensating advantage of interviewing the principal investigator of most of the projects under review. Since some different information was available to each team, the combined perspective has a distinct advantage over either separately.

The collaborative aspect of this evaluation study turned out well. Collaboration clearly contributed in terms of information. Collaboration also contributed to insight and assessment. But there were certain problems inherent in the collaborative aspects of the study as well. The geographic constraint of coordinating parallel efforts some 4500 miles apart was significant.

These then were some of the problems encountered in the evaluation effort. They were not trivial. They undoubtedly had an effect on the study as it ran its course. Some of the problems were anticipated, some were not. These problems should be kept in mind as the report is read. On balance we felt that the evaluation was reasonably successful and can be a positive influence on the decision-making process.

An Additional Consideration

The Special Foreign Currency Program is based on the availability of U.S.-owned foreign currency in excess of requirements as determined by the Treasury Department. In June 1971, when this study was commissioned, it was intended to assess the impact of the Special Foreign Currency Program in both the United States and Yugoslavia in order to provide for an improved program in the future. The parallel studies of impact in the two countries as designed by the Harvard team and the Yugoslavia team were specific to the Special Foreign Currency Program in Yugoslavia. The results of this evaluation effort and the information marshaled will undoubtedly serve best the purpose of improving decisions in the Special Foreign Currency Program in Yugoslavia. The value of the study is not limited to this context, however. Clearly there should be much in this report that has potential value to decision-makers in other Special Foreign Currency Programs, in other health research programs, other research programs, and in general program management.

The broader usefulness of this evaluation study has apparently assumed increased relevance in the past few months. The continued designation of Yugoslavia as an excess-currency country is apparently less certain now than it was when this study was initiated. The Harvard team and the Yugoslav team have recently learned, for example, that the cooperative research program in Yugoslavia could in the future be administered by a jointly sponsored binational foundation.

This study was designed as an evaluation of the existing program. It is clearly most relevant to that program. It is likely, however, that it can contribute to other programs as well.

2

The Special Foreign Currency Program in Historical Perspective

Introduction

The Special Foreign Currency Program is based on the availability of U.S.-owned foreign currency. The program is limited to so-called excess-currency countries. An excess-currency country is one in which the United States owns local currency in excess of its expected normal requirements for two fiscal years following the year in which the determination is made. The determination is made by the Treasury Department.

The central focus of this Yugoslav Evaluation Study, of course, is on the *use* of excess currencies for health research in one country. This focus is appropriate, since the generation of excess currencies is not within the province of the decision-makers for whom this evaluation study was completed.

Decisions made by policy-makers in the Special Foreign Currency Program do not in the normal course of events affect the generation of excess currencies. Their decisions, of course, are affected by the generation of excess currencies, since the program depends on their availability. Further, it is obvious, of course, that once excess currencies are generated, decisions within the Special Foreign Currency Program have a direct effect on availability over time.

While the evaluation was concentrated exclusively on the use of excess currencies for health research in Yugoslavia, an historical overview of the overall program does provide an appropriate perspective.

The Original P.L. 480 Program

The second session of the Eighty-third Congress passed the Agricultural Trade Development and Assistance Act of 1954. This act, Public Law 83-480, provided for the sale of U.S. agricultural commodities for nonconvertible currencies. According to the language of the legislation, the nonconvertible currencies were to be used by the U.S. "to expand international trade, to encourage economic development, to purchase strategic materials, to pay United States obligations abroad, to promote collective strength, and to foster in other ways the foreign policy of the United States."

A complete understanding of the purposes and operations of the Agricultural Trade Development and Assistance Act of 1954 requires an appreciation of the foreign policy legacy of the post-World War II era and the domestic and international agricultural conditions during the 1950s.

9

American foreign assistance in the immediate post-World War II years was concentrated in relief aid and the rehabilitation of economies severely damaged by the war. The European recovery program (Marshall Plan) included vast agricultural shipments, which served to stimulate American agricultural production. In the 1950s, as the revived European economies elected to conserve their limited dollar exchange reserves and bought agricultural commodities from neighboring countries on more favorable financial terms, significant agricultural surpluses accumulated in the United States.

The tensions of the Cold War era, and particularly the experience in Korea, dominated the direction of U.S. foreign assistance in the 1950s. With sizable economic commitments, American foreign-policy-makers sought to strengthen the economies of those countries sharing U.S. strategic objectives. American assistance programs were directed toward generating new markets and expanding international trade. With the success of the Marshall Plan in Europe, the emphasis of foreign assistance programs shifted to the emerging less-developed nations of the Third World. U.S.-sponsored programs of economic development assistance to these less-developed nations were designed to promote self-sustaining economic growth and to foster the evolution of mature democratic societies whose fundamental interests would be compatible with those of the U.S.

The objectives of disposing of agricultural surpluses and aiding less-developed countries reenforced each other in the P.L. 480 program. Farm surpluses were a perennial headache to successive administrations. A solution to this problem required the creation of new markets without disrupting the existing flow of agricultural products in international trade. The underdeveloped world offered these new markets. However, since dollar shortages in these countries precluded payments in hard currencies, recipient countries were allowed to pay the dollar equivalent in their own currencies.

The key to the enactment of P.L. 480 in 1954 was the growing stock of agricultural surpluses. A careful reading of the text of the law reveals that the disposal of surpluses was intended to generate new markets and to facilitate international trade. A review of the evolution of P.L. 480, however, reveals a variety of interests.

Agricultural surpluses were apparently viewed by the administration as a temporary phenomenon which required a quick solution. In his 1954 Budget Message, President Eisenhower "emphasized in connection with this program that it is purely temporary, predicated upon adoption of our domestic agricultural program which should not involve the continued accumulation of large surpluses." Originally the president had intended to dispose of surpluses in a finance relief program focused particularly in India and Pakistan. The Farm Bureau and the farm bloc in Congress were far more interested in the sale of these commodities in whatever currency, since relief aid had a tendency to grow out of proportion to the original commitment. Other members of Congress were concerned over the short-term aspects of such a program, for in a matter of obvious foreign-policy dimensions relief aid would be directly under the control of the Executive.

P.L. 480 seemed to reconcile all these interests. Not only would the program provide an orderly and gradual liquidation of these surpluses, but it would also expand consumption in areas where there existed a demonstrable underconsumption of foods essential to good nutrition. In addition, the sale of such commodities under conditions favorable to the recipient country spared the U.S. of criticism that it was dumping excess food supply on the world market.

Proceeds from local currency sales normally served two purposes. Approximately 20 percent of these currencies were used to pay U.S. obligations overseas. The remainder was at the disposal of the recipient country, albeit the U.S. held title to these currencies. By mutual agreement between the U.S. and the host country, these currencies were then used to fund development projects that would significantly contribute to the strengthening of the economy and improve the country's competitive position in the world market. An amendment of P.L. 480 did add a third purpose: some 5 percent of U.S.-owned local currency was set aside for loans to finance U.S. business investment in the host country.

During the Kennedy administration the permanence of agricultural surpluses was apparently recognized and a single agency, Food for Peace, was given jurisdiction over the program. Increased emphasis was given to the use of P.L. 480 as an instrument of foreign aid rather than as an agricultural program. Subsequent amendments to P.L. 480 deleted reference to U.S. surplus disposal, and it became U.S. policy to use this country's abundant agricultural productivity to combat hunger and malnutrition. In addition, it became part of U.S. policy to use its agricultural capacity to assist countries that were determined to improve their own agricultural production. U.S. foreign-aid policy seemed to move in the direction of a "self-help" program.

The local currency sales provision of P.L. 480 was intended to benefit the recipient country in its payments for agricultural commodities. Further, the loan of such local currency proceeds would be used to finance development projects. The loan was repayable in dollars at 3 percent, or it could be repaid in the local currency at 4 percent. Most repayments were accomplished in local currency. When the dollar began to come under pressure in international markets there was a subsequent reassessment of the local currency sales provision.

In the interest of preserving the integrity of the dollar, the goal of fostering economic development was somewhat frustrated. Since local currencies were used to pay U.S. personnel and cover U.S. obligations overseas, recipient countries had little access to dollars, and a normal dollar flow was essential to maintaining their foreign exchange position. Furthermore, the use of local currency proceeds from sales for the financing of development programs, and their subsequent repayment with interest, meant that the host country was dealing exclusively in its own currency. Such a situation did little to facilitate its activity in the world market, an avowed goal of the P.L. 480 program. For the

U.S., operations conducted only with local currencies and the interest derived from loans meant that the stock of U.S.-owned soft currencies was growing.

As the U.S. balance of payments worsened in the sixties, the accumulation of vast sums of soft currencies owned by the U.S. showed no signs of abating. The pressure to use P.L. 480 as a means of improving the balance-of-payments position intensified. Over time, amendments to the law were passed that increased the possible uses of local currencies generated by P.L. 480 agreements. Typically, these uses were tailored to reduce the necessity of obtaining local currencies by dollar payment in the process of executing official U.S. government activities. In 1959, provisions were added for dollar credit sales with long-term repayment periods. Beginning in 1966 credit sales were conducted under a new method that provided for installments to be paid either in dollars or, at the option of the U.S., in currencies that can be converted into dollars.

The year 1966 represented a turning point in the history of P.L. 480. In addition to the policy changes incorporated into the law, the structure of the law was revised considerably. In line with foreign-policy objectives, the programs undertaken with local currency funding had to demonstrate the effectiveness with which the country could use available resources—both internal and external—to promote economic and social development. It was argued that aid is most effective in bringing about the transition from dependence or stagnation to self-sustaining growth when it is concentrated in countries that are doing the most to help themselves. The insistence that transactions be conducted in convertible currencies allowed for long-term repayment at minimal interest rates. In this way, the host country would have more control over the movement of its own currency, while conducting more international business with hard, convertible currencies.

The Special Foreign Currency Program

The overview of the evolution of the P.L. 480 program outlined in the previous section does contribute to an understanding of the basic program. As the supply of U.S.-owned foreign currency increased, the Congress endorsed appropriations of these currencies to be used for several programs in scientific activities overseas. Health research was one of the first such scientific activities in the expanded-use dimension of the overall program.

The Eighty-sixth Congress passed the International Health Research Act of 1960, Public Law 86-610. The legislation stipulated two objectives:

1. To advance the status of the health sciences in the United States and thereby the health of the American people through cooperative endeavors with other countries in health research, research training; and
2. To advance the international status of the health sciences through cooperative enterprises in health research, research planning, and research training.

The Surgeon General has authorization to pursue the first objective; the second may be pursued at the discretion of the president.

The health research program derives its legislative authority to use excess foreign currencies generated by P.L. 480 sales from amendments to P.L. 480 under Section 104k, and under Sections 3 and 4 of the International Health Research Act, which additionally permits utilization of excess foreign currencies accruing to the U.S. from the repayment of development loans and other activities.

The Public Health Service received its first congressional appropriation under these acts, an amount of some $3.7 million, in fiscal 1961. This was the beginning of the Special Foreign Currency Program—although in the early years the program was referred to as the P.L. 480 program.

The congressional appropriation to the Special Foreign Currency Program in the Public Health Service grew to some $9 million in fiscal 1962, then dropped to an average of less than half that amount for the next four years. This resulted from the difficulty in arranging for research projects to use the appropriated but unspent monies. By fiscal 1967, project solicitation channels resulted in a steady stream of appropriate research proposals. The appropriation rose to $10 million that year and to $15 million for the next two years. Confusion in the Department of Health, Education, and Welfare and the Congress resulted in a drastic cut in the program budget to $3.5 million in fiscal 1970 as both parties apparently thought they were saving dollars. Clarification of this issue and the funding of a backlog of projects led to an appropriation of some $32 million in fiscal 1971. The budget of the Special Foreign Currency Program has been at a level of some $26 million for the past two years.

The Special Foreign Currency Program has been in operation for thirteen years and presently involves NIH, HSMHA, and FDA. Overall program and budget coordination is currently the responsibility of the Office of International Health.

Over the years twelve countries have participated in the health research program. Since its inception in fiscal 1961, this international research program has grown in size and in scope. Special Foreign Currency Program obligations by country are outlined in Table 2-1.

The international health research program is quite small relative to the yearly operating budgets of the participating agencies. Nevertheless, it can provide a valuable alternative resource for the achievement of domestic health objectives. Given constraints upon the availability of dollars for the support of scientific activities, both in the United States and abroad, the utilization of excess foreign currencies is a valuable resource. Since a variety of important and unique research opportunities of potential usefulness exists in excess currency countries, the Special Foreign Currency Program is capable of developing knowledge and insights that might not otherwise be forthcoming.

Mutuality of interest, coordination, and responsiveness to the health goals and priorities of both the United States and the host country are intended to be

Table 2-1
Special Foreign Currency Program Obligations by Country, Fiscal Year 1961-Fiscal Year 1972

					Fiscal Year				
	1961-64	1965	1966	1967	1968	1969	1970	1971	1972 (Estimated)
Brazil	$ 65,534	$ (1,136)	–	–	–	–	–	–	–
Burma	481,897	6,304	$ (5,000)	$ (15,003)	$ (24)	–	–	–	–
Ceylon	–	–	–	2,343	6,032	–	–	–	–
Guinea	–	–	–	–	–	–	–	–	$ 50,000
India	2,687,156	438,804	2,210,232	1,369,876	1,898,205	$4,473,631	$ (186,855)	$ 6,045,078	6,203,762
Israel	3,303,893	1,668,110	1,443,348	3,380,803	5,435,382	198,636	2,513,464	2,091,000	64,000
Morocco	–	–	–	–	–	1,163	902	1,075,000	415,000
Pakistan	1,805,396	1,171,480	183,240	1,277,758	2,194,890	3,276,072	38,048	2,728,417	1,759,738
Poland	2,917,276	640,879	1,113,006	1,575,104	1,473,390	1,647,747	(532,203)	4,993,420	7,395,555
Tunisia	–	–	–	250	127,164	564,409	85,745	1,970,805	942,050
U.A.R. (Egypt)	953,856	951,085	1,712,526	861,093	(47,902)	657,050	(100,212)	1,334,591	1,375,100
Yugoslavia	1,216,776	173,429	492,612	773,563	2,323,928	5,972,928	1,230,195	8,996,689	7,339,795
Total	13,431,784	4,848,955	7,149,964	9,225,787	13,411,065	16,791,636	3,049,084	29,235,000	25,545,000

Source: Hearings before House Appropriations Subcommittee, FY 1971-1972, Thursday, April 22, 1971.

the principal characteristics of the health research program under the Special Foreign Currency Program. Currently, program activities are focused on problems of nutrition, population and family planning, disease prevention and control, the organization and delivery of health services, development of health manpower, and environmental health. Budget estimates for fiscal year 1971 indicate that the international research program will concentrate significant funding on projects dealing with health care delivery systems, environmental health, and population and family planning. This emphasis appears to be consonant with U.S. domestic health priorities.

Gauging the Domestic Health Priorities of the United States

The United States does not have a national health policy. There is no clear, well-defined, delineated set of objectives and priorities. That is not to say that goals and objectives do not exist, or that the nation does not undertake health programs consistent with implicit priorities. Rather, the objectives and priorities have to be inferred from a variety of statements, documents, actions, and program activities.

As described in the previous section, a primary purpose of the Special Foreign Currency Program is to contribute to the achievement of domestic health goals. Hence, to view the program in context or to assess the impact of the program in this regard it is first necessary to define and specify the domestic health objectives. The list of domestic health objectives of the United States outlined in Table 2-2 was derived to serve this purpose.

Table 2-2
Domestic Health Objectives of the United States

1. Curing diseases and organic dysfunctions or impairments.
2. Morbidity reduction.
3. Preventive health care advances.
4. Promotion of a positive health life (e.g., consumer education and nutritional improvements).
5. Improved geriatric care and degenerative disease reduction.
6. Improved treatment for mental disorders.
7. Efficient health services delivery: institutional improvements, more efficient manpower use, and increased manpower.
8. Equitable and efficient costing arrangements.
9. Solutions to the problems raised by the secular societal trends of industrialization, urbanization, population growth, and environmental impairment.
10. Improved health information exchange and statistical methods.

The list is actually a form of summary. It draws heavily upon such statements as *Health Goals for the Nation* (1961), *Toward a Social Report* (1969), and *Towards a Comprehensive Health Policy for the 1970's: A White Paper* (1971). The actual definition and specification of goals as represented by the list derived also benefited from reviews of other relevant literature, congressional actions, health agency budgets, and particularly from a series of interviews with individuals in key policy positions.

The relative emphasis upon the various objectives has shifted over the past decade. The ordering of the list should not be viewed as representing precedence or importance but simply convenience.

This list of domestic health objectives was derived to facilitate the evaluation study that is the subject of this report. The paramount concern was to obtain a relatively short working list that could be used in individual project evaluation. As such it provides a format for a description of project results and objectives, but not for a precise quantification of project benefits. In light of the shifting emphasis given to each of the objectives, such quantification would be impossible. It would not be feasible, for example, to state definitively whether the precise worth of a project should be gauged against the priorities prevailing when the enabling legislation was passed, when the project was approved, while it operated, when it was evaluated, or when the evaluative results guide further research. What it does allow, however, is quite meaningful and useful. Given such a list of health objectives, a knowledgeable reviewer can indicate his assessment of the relative impact a particular project has had or may have on any or all of the specific objectives. Such information should be of value to a decision-maker who is in a position to reflect on relative priorities.

This chapter was designed to present an overview of the Special Foreign Currency Program to focus the relevant perspective of the evaluation study. The program in Yugoslavia is viewed in some detail in the next chapter.

3

The Special Foreign Currency Program in Yugoslavia

Introduction

The use of excess currency funds for scientific research in Yugoslavia began in 1960. After a rather slow start it has grown substantially in both size and scope in recent years. The growth of the program is reflected in the summary of active projects outlined in Table 3-1.

The program consisted of a single project in 1960 and 1961. A second project was funded in 1962 and a third project was added in 1963. The program increased by three projects in 1964 and again in 1965. In 1966, three projects started and one project ended so that at the end of the first seven years the program consisted of only eleven active projects.

The data in Table 3-1 reflect a rather dramatic increase in the size and scope of the program from 1967 on. Seven, fifteen, and seventeen new projects were added to the program in 1967, 1968, and 1969 respectively. Only eight new projects were funded in 1970, occasioned by the apparent misunderstanding of the excess currency nature of the program, outlined in Chapter 2. In 1971, forty-nine new projects were funded. (Since the figure for 1971 is inflated by the backlog from 1970, the trend is perhaps better represented by taking the two years together.) Thus, of the 108 projects funded over the period 1960 through 1971, 12 were funded during the first seven years and 96 were funded during the last five years.

The same summary data are outlined in Table 3-2 by agency. These data indicate that the several agencies parallel the aggregate trend in program growth. These data also indicate significant differences among agency program sizes. Although NIH funded projects earlier, HSMHA's program has grown more rapidly, and by 1971 HSMHA had funded more than twice as many projects, 68 to 32. FDA funded only 7 of the 108 projects.[a]

In order to provide an overview of the program it is necessary to look briefly at the processes of project solicitation, approval, and funding. Additional insight is available from certain summary information, such as what kinds of research projects tend to be supported, what levels of support are provided by the U.S. and by Yugoslavia, and other administrative information.

---

[a]A small number of projects were funded in Yugoslavia by components of HEW that were later transfered to the Environmental Protection Agency. One project was completed prior to the establishment of the EPA and was included in the evaluation, but it is not to be thought of as constituting an EPA program.

Table 3-1
Summary of Special Foreign Currency Program in Yugoslavia, Number of Active Projects, 1960-71

Year	New Projects Funded	Projects Completed	Total Active Projects
1960	1	0	1
1961	0	0	1
1962	1	0	2
1963	1	0	3
1964	3	0	6
1965	3	0	9
1966	3	1	11
1967	7	0	18
1968	15	1	32
1969	17	1	48
1970	8	4	52
1971	49	8	93
	108	15	

Project Solicitation and Approval

There is no set mode for the solicitation of research proposals in Yugoslavia. The several agencies are encouraged to make use of whatever channels they find most effective. It is clear that over time a number of mechanisms have served to contribute to the flow of project proposals. The Federal Bureau for International Scientific, Educational, Cultural, and Technical Cooperation (FAISECTC) in Yugoslavia has had a central role in coordinating the flow of proposals and has served to publicize the program. Scientist-to-scientist contacts have served quite effectively in some cases to bring attention to the program and have resulted in many project proposals. On a number of occasions, agency personnel have traveled to Yugoslavia and communicated program interests to Yugoslav officials and scientists directly.

The mechanisms employed to publicize the program undoubtedly have an influence on the pattern of the flow of proposals. Scientist-to-scientist contacts are more likely to stimulate proposals from individual university-based researchers. Contacts between government officials in Yugoslavia and the U.S. are more likely to stimulate proposals from government institutes.

Whatever the source of the stimulation, once a proposal is initiated it flows through the same channels. The proposals must first be approved at the regional and federal levels in Yugoslavia, then they are forwarded to the American Embassy. (Apparently federal approval in Yugoslavia has been a formality in

Table 3-2
Summary of Special Foreign Currency Program in Yugoslavia by Agency, Number of Active Projects, 1960-71

Year	NIH		HSMHA		FDA		EPA		Total	
	New Projects Funded	Total Active Projects	New Projects Funded	Total Active Projects	New Projects Funded	Total Active Projects	New Projects Funded	Total Active Projects	New Projects Funded	Total Active Projects
1960	1	1	0	0	0	0	0	0	1	1
1961	0	1	0	0	0	0	0	0	0	1
1962	1	2	0	0	0	0	0	0	1	2
1963	0	2	1	1	0	0	0	0	1	3
1964	0	2	3	4	0	0	0	0	3	6
1965	0	2	3	7	0	0	0	0	3	9
1966	2	4	1	7	0	0	0	0	3	11
1967	0	4	7	14	0	0	0	0	7	18
1968	3	7	12	25	0	0	0	0	15	32
1969	2	9	13	37	2	2	0	0	17	48
1970	3	12	3	37	1	3	1	1	8	52[a]
1971	20	30	25	56	4	7	0	0	49	93

[a]The EPA project was funded for a three-month period and hence was not active at the end of 1970.

recent years.) The proposals then are transmitted through the Department of State (DOS) to the Office of International Health (OIH) and the relevant agencies.

Typically, the projects do not have American project officers at this stage. Particularly for projects with promise, the agencies attempt to persuade an American scientist to serve as project officer. Often the search for project officers is made difficult by the reluctance of department heads to excuse their personnel from full responsibility for their domestic duties. If a project officer is not found within an agency, one may be sought extramurally. The National Institutes of Health (NIH) has resorted most often to extramural project officers, yet there is feeling within the agency that projects with potential are sometimes lost because not enough project officers can be found. The first function of the project officer is to rewrite the proposal to put it in the format and language of domestic research proposals.

The intra-agency review processes differ among the agencies and among the departments. The review process of NIH is the best documented, but even it has its ambiguities and apparently does not always conform to its documentation. Every NIH project apparently undergoes two phases of Institute review: the first for scientific merit, the second for scientific merit and a consideration of project relevance and priority within the Institute. Study sections are convened to assess the scientific merit of extramural projects while intra-Institute committees often suffice for intramural projects. The study sections typically consist of six scientists. Institute review may consist of no more than certification by an ad hoc committee. It might be inferred that this review level often is perfunctory. At one time it was suggested to the evaluation team that a special advisory council provided the second review, but subsequently it was made clear that in fact it passed only upon those projects requiring supplementary hard currency funding. The Institute director certifies that a dual review has occurred and that the project is of relevance to the Institute before signing it and sending it to the Fogarty International Center.

The Fogarty Center must reconcile discrepancies among the previous reviews. It can also pass judgment upon the relevance of the project to agency objectives, and review adequacy and priority of the project. This review is performed by the director. He has the responsibility of bringing the approved funding into line with the level of the agency allotment assigned by the Office of International Health. The Fogarty Center tends to implement NIH's preference for intramural projects by assigning them priority over the extramural. The Center also tends to give priority to continuing projects over new ones. From the Fogarty Center, extramural projects go to the associate director for Extramural Research and Training, and intramural projects to the associate director for Direct Research at NIH. Both proposal types are finally reviewed by the deputy director for Science and the director of NIH. The agency level reviews further attest to the adequacy of previous reviews and confirm that the projects conform to NIH policies, procedures, and mission.

The review procedures of HSMHA and FDA are sufficiently similar that they can be outlined together. When high-quality proposals arrive from Yugoslavia, American project officers—virtually always members of the intramural staff—are assigned to them. The project officers may have to direct substantial rewriting of the proposals. The finished proposals undergo peer reviews consisting of at least three scientists. After receiving approval from the bureau heads in FDA and the department heads in HSMHA, the proposals are directed to the international program head of each agency, who check upon the adequacy of the previous reviews and occasionally reconcile conflicting reviews. They apparently can delay project approvals indefinitely. However, the main power they exercise over the divisions of their agencies is in their allocation of the agency budget. The heads of the divisions of both agencies make additional decisions as to which of the approved projects are actually funded from the division allocation.

Certain projects undergo special approval processes. All studies in the FDA that involve experimentation with humans must be reviewed by the Risk Committee to determine the hazard involved. When jurisdictional disputes arise—whether between agencies, or between the divisions of one agency—higher-level arbitrators are involved in resolving them.

From the agencies the proposals go to the Department of State, where a check is made to identify any projects that might have detrimental effects upon our foreign relations. Since the proposals pass many times over the desks of DOS, its input to the review process can occur at any time, but most often follows agency approval. The desk officer for the SFCP country has primary responsibility for the DOS review, but the embassies, the regional desk officers, and the Agency for International Development can be occasionally involved. No Yugoslav projects have been negatively reviewed at the DOS level.

The Funding Process

The agency heads of the Special Foreign Currency Program begin their budget preparation by soliciting from departments their anticipated project totals. These totals must be trimmed so that the agency total conforms to the estimates made in the five-year plan. HSMHA, for one, tends to trim by applying the rule of thumb of equal percentage cuts across the board. OIH makes the determination of which of the five-year-plan totals it chooses to meet in any given fiscal year. When recently OIH chose to defend the low forecast figure it necessitated difficult cuts by the agency program heads in the departmental budgets.

The entire OIH budget is scrutinized by the Office of the Secretary of HEW before the Department sends its own budget on to the Office of Management and Budget (OMB) and the Congress. Though SFCP personnel now take these latter approval levels for granted, it should be noted that as recently as fiscal year 1970, the OIH Special Foreign Currency Program budget was substantially cut. This cut resulted from the failure of the Office of the Secretary of HEW, OMB, and the Congress to realize that the SFCP did not obligate dollars.

The budget that OIH prepares for OMB breaks down the counterpart currency requirements by country. The budget approved by Congress and signed by the president does not make these distinctions, and OIH is not bound by the estimates it has presented to OMB. The agency program heads can generally spend their budgetary allotments in any of the SFCP countries. Only for countries in which counterpart funds are in tight supply is stricter OMB supervision required, in the form of quarterly apportionment reports from OIH.

The appropriations for the SFCP are no-year monies. They may be dispensed in any year after that of the budget in which they appear. NIH, however, has a policy that no projects are funded for more than three years. HMSHA and FDA projects have no such limitations. The complete funding for the period covered by the project agreement is provided in the initial project appropriation. For projects that it anticipates will last for more than three years, NIH may sign the original agreement upon the tacit understanding that it will be renewed. Even in these cases, the renewal proposal must undergo the complete NIH review.

A problem that plagues all Yugoslav projects but is most serious in the case of the longer agreements is that of inflationary cost overruns. Neither the agencies nor OIH has a set policy here, although the tendency has been to go along with the documented requests of the principal investigators. Special problems arise in the case of the Yugoslav devaluations. The standard macroeconomic concept of devaluation is that it leaves internal services rendered and value added unchanged. The costs of imported laboratory equipment naturally rise but salaries theoretically remain constant. OIH has accordingly denied the requests of principal investigators for across-the-board budgetary increases equal to the percentage of devaluation. Yet it is undeniable that internal salary inflation accompanies the devaluations. OIH has an unenviable task in trying to determine just how much inflationary increases are justified. It has recently attempted to obtain measures of local price levels to determine the legitimacy of requests for increases, but found the task of data collection too great. There is no automatic elasticity in the budgets to cover inflationary overruns.

When a project has been approved for funding an agreement is drawn; when the agreement has been signed by both sides the project officially begins. As the data in Tables 3-1 and 3-2 indicated, 108 projects were started in the years 1960 through 1971. During the first six months of 1972, two additional projects were started; a number of others are approved for funding, but their actual starts were pending final signatures. The 110 projects that officially started through June 1972 form the basis for the rest of this evaluation report.

**Project Classification—The Kinds
of Activities Funded**

The 110 projects have been classified by the type of research or major activity undertaken. This classification is outlined in some detail in Table 3-3. The same information is summarized in less detail in Table 3-4.

Table 3-3

Classification of Projects by Type of Research or Major Activity by Agency

Project Type	Agency				
	NIH	HSMHA	FDA	EPA	Total
Laboratory research	18	1	2	–	21
Laboratory and clinical research	1	2	2	–	5
Laboratory, clinical and epidemiological research	–	2	–	–	2
Laboratory and epidemiological research	1	5	1	–	7
Laboratory research and conference	1	–	–	–	1
Clinical research	1	6	–	–	7
Clinical and epidemiological research	1	10	2	–	13
Clinical and epidemiological research and student exchange	–	1	–	–	1
Epidemiological research	3	22	–	–	25
Epidemiological research, manpower training, and other	–	1	–	–	1
Epidemiological research and other	–	1	–	–	1
Conference	1	9	–	1	11
Manpower training	–	3	–	–	3
Student exchange	–	3	–	–	3
Translations	1	–	–	–	1
Critical reviews	4	–	–	–	4
Other	–	4	–	–	4
Total	32	70	7	1	110

Laboratory research, clinical research, epidemiological research, and combinations of two or more of these types of research are the major activity of the majority of the 110 projects. Twenty-one projects are essentially laboratory research projects. An additional fifteen projects involve laboratory research as a significant aspect of the overall project. Seven projects are primarily clinical research projects. Twenty-one projects combine clinical research with some other activity. Twenty-five projects are classified as epidemiological research, and an additional twenty-five projects include a significant epidemiological component.

There are, of course, rather significant differences among the agencies. Laboratory research projects represent the dominant activity of the NIH program. Clinical research and epidemiological research tend to be the dominant activities of the HSMHA program. The much smaller FDA program—only seven

Table 3-4

Summary of Classification of Projects by Type of Research or Major Activity by Agency

Project Type	Agency				Total
	NIH	HSMHA	FDA	EPA	
Laboratory research	21	10	5	–	36
Clinical research	3	21	4	–	28
Epidemiological research	5	42	3	–	50
Conference	2	9	–	1	12
Manpower training	–	4	–	–	4
Student exchange	–	4	–	–	4
Translations	1	–	–	–	1
Critical reviews	4	–	–	–	4
Other	–	6	–	–	6

projects in all—appears to be roughly balanced among laboratory, clinical, and epidemiological research. These characteristics of the Special Foreign Currency Program Activities in Yugoslavia seem consistent with the nature and objectives of the three agencies.

After laboratory, clinical, and epidemiological research, conferences represent the largest number of projects. Ten percent of all projects, 11 of 110, were conferences. (A twelfth project included a conference as a major activity.) The conference as a project type is somewhat unique to HSMHA. Nine of the eleven conferences were sponsored by HSMHA.

Finally, there are areas with fewer projects. HSMHA has sponsored a small number of projects that involve manpower training as a major activity and student exchange programs that involve sending American medical students to Yugoslavia. NIH has sponsored four projects that are designed to provide critical reviews of literature and one project that was designed to provide a translation of three Yugoslav medical journals into English. The latter project was actually initiated by the National Library of Medicine in 1960.

The Level of U.S. Financial Support

To this point, the Special Foreign Currency Program in Yugoslavia has been reviewed in terms of the number of projects. The program should also be reviewed in terms of the level of financial support. U.S. financial support over time and the levels of financial support provided the different types of projects are considered in this section. Yugoslav financial contributions to SFCP projects will be reviewed in the next section.

Table 3-5

Summary of Special Foreign Currency Program Budgets in Yugoslavia, 1960-72

| Year | Number of Projects | Excess Currency Funds | | Percentage Increase |
		Originally Budgeted (in dollars)	Budgeted to Date (in dollars)	
1960	1	295,878	742,378	150.9
1961	–	–	–	–
1962	1	450,000	782,088	73.8
1963	1	99,194	246,000	148.0
1964	3	394,878	796,678	101.8
1965	3	338,871	1,524,741	349.9
1966	3	323,634	681,976	110.7
1967	7	663,695	1,371,001	106.6
1968	15	2,012,597	3,943,924	96.0
1969	17	4,412,652	5,529,415	25.3
1970	8	806,557	1,160,966	43.9
1971	49	7,869,712	7,878,995	0.1
1972	2	370,943	370,943	0.0
Program totals	110	18,038,611	25,029,105	38.8

The data in Table 3-5 provide an overview of the level of financial support over time of the entire Special Foreign Currency Program in Yugoslavia. The number of projects initially funded in a given year is listed in the first column. The amount of excess currency funds originally budgeted for the projects started in a given year is listed in the second column. The amount eventually budgeted to date for the projects started in a given year is listed in the third column. Finally, the percentage increases in the funds budgeted to date over the original amounts budgeted are listed in the fourth column.

These data provide a number of insights. First, of course, the relative growth of the Special Foreign Currency Program is clearly reflected in the levels of financial support. From 1960 to 1966 the amount of financial support originally budgeted for the program averaged less than $300,000. In 1967, the amount of original support was more than double the previous average, at some $663,695. In 1968, the level of original support more than tripled, to an amount in excess of $2 million. The level doubled again in 1969 to some $4.4 million. After a decline to less than a million dollars in 1970, original financial support for the program rose to $7.9 million in 1971. (Since the 1971 amount is inflated by the backlog from 1970, the average of the two perhaps better reflects the trend. The average original budget of 1970 and 1971, $4.3 million, is approximately the same as that of 1969.) These data reflect the relatively slow start of the Special

Foreign Currency Program in Yugoslavia, the rather dramatic increase in its size and scope beginning in 1967, and an apparent leveling off of the program growth in the last few years.

Second, the data in Table 3-5 indicate the propensity for the projects funded under the Special Foreign Currency Program in Yugoslavia to be amended. Certainly the amounts originally budgeted were not sufficient indicators of the program's eventual expenditures. Amended budgets tend to be the rule rather than the exception. The amount of funds allocated to date for projects started between 1960 and 1968 has often ranged from twice to more than four times that originally budgeted. This characteristic of the program is clearly indicated by the percentage increase in the budget to date over the original budget for projects started in a given year; 73.8 was the lowest percentage increase over the original budget for projects started in a given year from 1960 through 1968. The somewhat lower percentage increase over the original budget for projects started in the most recent years may reflect a change in trend, but it is more likely simply due to the fact that these projects have not yet completed their original time period, and hence have not yet been candidates for amendment.

Finally, to the extent that the lower percentage increases over the original budgets for projects started in recent years are due to the fact that they are relatively new projects, these figures might be expected to increase over time. In any event, the financial characteristics of projects that started in earlier years are not quite comparable to those of projects that started in later years.

The level of financial support over time is outlined by agency in Table 3-6. The first four columns of this table include the same budgetary information for each of the four agencies as the corresponding columns of Table 3-5 included for the overall program. In addition, Table 3-6 includes data on average project length. Since no agency funded new projects in each year, entries are only included in Table 3-6 for years in which an agency funded new projects.

It is apparent from these data that there are rather significant differences among the agencies. Perhaps most striking is the fact that new NIH projects did not really contribute to the rapid growth in the level of financial support from 1967 to 1969. In fact, NIH did not fund any new projects in 1967, and the original budget totals for 1968 and 1969 were somewhat lower than those of previous years.

HSMHA alone appears to have contributed to the rapid growth of the Special Foreign Currency Program in Yugoslavia from 1967 to 1969. It was over this three-year period that HSMHA assumed its dominant role in the overall program. Through 1966, HSMHA had funded eight projects, at an original budget level of some $991,343 and NIH had funded four projects, at an original budget level of some $910,878. But from 1967 through 1969 HSMHA funded thirty-two new projects, at an original budget level of some $6.5 million, while NIH was funding only five new projects, at an original budget level of only $238,589.

The original budget data for projects started in a given year are not indicative of the actual agency budgets for that year. The actual budgets tended to be higher, of course, because they often included allocations for projects started in earlier years. In fact, however, the proportions of the aggregate program over the entire period 1960-62 reflect essentially the same image as the original budget data. Of the some $25 million in excess-currency funds budgeted to date for support of SFCP projects in Yugoslavia, HSMHA projects have accounted for some $18.9 million, NIH projects for some $4.8 million, FDA projects for $1.3 million; and the single EPA project involved only $54,000.

The data in Table 3-6 seem to indicate that the propensity to amend projects and to increase the level of expenditures significantly over the amounts originally budgeted is rather common among the agencies. Certainly it is the case for both NIH and HSMHA. The percentage increase in the budget to date over the original budget for projects started in the years 1960 through 1969 by NIH have ranged from 73.8 to 163.6 percent. The range is somewhat wider in the case of HSMHA, but the same pattern prevails. In fact, the percentage increase of budget to date over the original budget for the entire program was some 35.5 percent for NIH and some 43.2 percent for HSMHA, even though 20 of the 32 NIH projects and 27 of the 70 HSMHA projects had virtually the same budget to date and original budget because they had started so recently.

Budgets increase either because of an increase in the amount allocated to a project per year, or because of an amended longer project life, or both. The data in Table 3-6 suggest that both project length and the amount expended per year have tended to increase for projects funded by both NIH and HSMHA. The FDA program is of such recent vintage that it is not really comparable to the older programs of NIH and HSMHA. Yet even in the case of FDA, the increase in budget to date over original budget for projects started in 1969 has been 9 percent.

Tables 3-7 and 3-8 are included to provide additional perspectives on the size of project budgets and the length of projects, respectively. These data suggest additional significant differences among the several agencies. NIH projects tend to have total budgets that cluster toward the lower end of the distribution. Twenty-seven of the thirty-two NIH projects have budgets of less than $300,000 and no fewer than twenty-two have budgets of less than $100,000. The median budget of NIH projects is only some $69,664.

The budgets of HSMHA projects display a quite different pattern. Proportionately fewer HSMHA projects have budgets at the lower end of the distribution. In fact, slightly more than half of all HSMHA projects have budgets in excess of $200,000; and at $212,383, the median budget of HSMHA projects is more than three times the median budget of NIH projects.

The seven FDA projects display a tighter distribution than those of the two larger agencies. Six of the seven FDA projects have budgets between $100,000 and $300,000. The median budget of FDA projects is $203,433.

The differences among the agencies in terms of project length are even more

Table 3-6
Summary of Yugoslav Special Foreign Currency Program Budgets and Project Lengths by Agency, 1960-72

Year	Number of Projects	Original Budget (in dollars)	Budget to Date (in dollars)	Percentage Increase	Average Project Length	
					Original (in years)	Current (in years)
NIH						
1960	1	295,878	742,378	150.9	12.0	12.0
1962	1	450,000	782,088	73.8	5.0	9.0
1966	2	165,234	435,510	163.6	3.0	6.0
1968	3	149,624	282,041	88.5	3.0	5.0
1969	2	88,965	162,363	82.5	2.0	3.0
1970	3	283,941	294,410	3.7	3.0	3.0
1971	20	2,134,612	2,134,612	0.0	3.0	3.0
NIH Totals	32	3,568,254	4,833,402	35.5	3.3	3.8
HSMHA						
1963	1	99,194	246,000	148.0	2.0	10.0
1964	3	394,878	796,678	101.8	4.3	7.0
1965	3	338,871	1,524,741	349.9	3.0	6.0
1966	1	158,400	246,466	55.6	3.0	4.0
1967	7	663,695	1,371,001	106.6	3.9	4.9
1968	12	1,862,973	3,661,883	96.6	2.9	4.6
1969	13	3,994,207	5,007,771	25.4	3.4	4.3
1970	3	371,250	713,726	92.2	2.7	3.7
1971	25	4,917,435	4,926,718	0.2	3.7	3.7
1972	2	370,943	370,943	0.0	4.0	4.0
HSMHA Totals	70	13,171,846	18,865,927	43.2	3.5	4.4

FDA						
1969	2	329,480	359,281	9.0	5.0	5.0
1970	1	97,366	98,830	1.5	3.0	3.0
1971	4	817,665	817,665	0.0	2.8	2.8
FDA Totals	7	1,244,511	1,275,776	2.5	3.4	3.4
EPA						
1970	1	54,000	54,000	0.0	1.0	1.0
EPA Totals	1	54,000	54,000	0.0	1.0	1.0
Program Totals	110	18,038,611	25,029,105	38.8	3.4	4.2

Table 3-7

Distribution of Project Budgets by Amount of Budget to Date by Agency

Total Budget to Date (in dollars)	Number of Projects				
	NIH	HSMHA	FDA	EPA	Total
Under 100,000	22	18	1	1	42
100,000-199,999	5	16	2	–	23
200,000-299,999	2	11	4	–	17
300,000-399,999	–	12	–	–	12
400,000-499,999	–	5	–	–	5
500,000-599,999	–	–	–	–	–
600,000-699,999	–	3	–	–	3
700,000-799,999	2	2	–	–	4
800,000-899,999	–	1	–	–	1
900,000-999,999	1	–	–	–	1
1,000,000-1,199,000	–	2	–	–	2
	32	70	7	1	110
Median budget	$69,664	$212,383	$203,433	$54,000	$136,603

Table 3-8

Distribution of Project Length by Number of Years Approved to Date by Agency

Project Length in Years	Number of Projects				
	NIH	HSMHA	FDA	EPA	Total
1	–	8	–	1	9
2	1	3	1	–	5
3	25	9	4	–	38
4	–	13	1	–	14
5	–	24	–	–	24
6	4	6	1	–	11
7	–	1	–	–	1
8	–	2	–	–	2
9	1	2	–	–	3
10	–	2	–	–	2
11	–	–	–	–	–
12	1	–	–	–	1
	32	70	7	1	110
Median project length in years	3	5	3	1	4

striking. Actually, the distributions of project length of NIH and FDA are quite similar, but that of HSMHA is quite different. HSMHA does in fact support longer projects than any other agency. This characteristic can be inferred from a comparison of either the several distributions of project length or the median project lengths in years. The projects of NIH and FDA are only 60 percent as long as those of HSMHA, on average.

The data reviewed to this point have suggested several differences among the agencies that participate in the Special Foreign Currency Program. The data outlined in this section indicate that HSMHA projects have the largest budgets and last for the longest periods of time, on average. FDA projects have budgets closer in size to those of HSMHA, but closer in length to those of NIH. The classification of projects by type outlined in the previous section showed rather significant differences among the agencies in terms of the kinds of projects they tend to sponsor. NIH tends to concentrate on laboratory research projects. Clinical research and epidemiological research tend to be the dominant activities of the HSMHA program. The relatively small FDA program tends to be balanced among laboratory, clinical, and epidemiological research. In order to assess the extent to which these several phenomena are related, it is necessary to consider the levels of financial support provided the several types of projects. The level and length of financial support by type of research or major activity is summarized in Table 3-9 for the overall program. The same data are outlined by agency in Table 3-10.

By far the most money is spent for epidemiological research. Some $10.8 million or 43 percent of the total budget to date of the Special Foreign Currency Program in Yugoslavia has been devoted to epidemiological research. Clinical and epidemiological research at $2.9 million; laboratory research at $1.8 million; laboratory and epidemiological research at $1.6 million; and clinical research at $1.2 million follow. These five types of research activities have accounted for almost 75 percent of the total budget to date of the Special Foreign Currency Program in Yugoslavia.

The most expensive project types in terms of average budget per project were rather unique. The project designed to translate three Yugoslav medical journals into English had a total budget of some $742,378. The manpower-training and other projects with a total budget of some $718,417 involved the funding of a new institute designed to carry out special population studies in the social and biological sciences. But several less unique project types were characterized by relatively high average total budgets per project; and included individual projects with total budgets that exceeded those of the translation project and the funding of the special institute.

The twenty-five epidemiological research projects had an average total budget per project of some $431,435, which was almost double the average total budget per project of the overall program—$227,537. The implication of these data is clearly that epidemiological research is a relatively expensive undertaking.

Table 3-9

Summary of Level and Length of Financial Support by Type of Research or Major Activity

Project Type	Number of Projects	Total Budget to Date (in dollars)	Average Project Length (in years)	Average Budget to Date	
				Per Project (in dollars)	Per Project Per Year (in dollars)
Laboratory research	21	1,835,051	3.5	87,383	25,137
Laboratory and clinical research	5	745,129	3.4	149,145	43,831
Laboratory, clinical and epidemiological research	2	771,945	4.0	385,973	96,493
Laboratory and epidemiological research	7	1,563,685	5.0	223,383	44,676
Laboratory research and conference	1	279,422	6.0	279,422	46,570
Clinical research	7	1,236,272	4.4	176,610	39,879
Clinical and epidemiological research	13	2,882,197	5.0	221,707	44,341
Clinical and epidemiological research and student exchange	1	242,362	5.0	242,362	80,787
Epidemiological research	25	10,785,877	4.8	431,435	89,139
Epidemiological research, manpower training and other	1	718,417	4.0	718,417	179,604
Epidemiological research and other	1	607,500	4.0	607,500	151,875
Conference	11	776,006	1.8	70,546	38,800
Manpower training	3	241,957	3.0	80,652	26,884
Student exchange	3	652,807	6.7	217,602	32,640
Translations	1	742,378	12.0	742,378	61,865
Critical reviews	4	70,038	2.8	17,510	6,367
Other	4	878,062	4.0	219,515	54,878
Total	110	25,029,105	4.2	227,537	54,768

Table 3-10
Summary of Level and Length of Financial Support by Type of Research or Major Activity by Agency

Project Type	Number of Projects	Total Budget to Date (in dollars)	Average Project Length (in years)	Average Budget to Date	
				Per Project (in dollars)	Per Project Per Year (in dollars)
NIH					
Laboratory research	18	1,495,148	3.5	83,063	23,733
Laboratory and clinical research	1	23,743	3.0	23,743	7,914
Laboratory and epidemiological research	1	56,922	3.0	56,922	18,974
Laboratory research and conference	1	279,422	6.0	279,422	46,570
Clinical research	1	249,735	3.0	249,735	83,245
Clinical and epidemiological research	1	30,741	3.0	30,741	10,247
Epidemiological research	3	1,795,442	5.0	598,481	119,696
Conference	1	89,833	3.0	89,833	29,944
Translations	1	742,378	12.0	742,378	61,865
Critical reviews	4	70,038	2.8	17,510	6,367
NIH Totals	32	4,833,402	3.5	151,044	39,618

Table 3-10 (cont.)

Project Type	Number of Projects	Total Budget to Date (in dollars)	Average Project Length (in years)	Average Budget to Date	
				Per Project (in dollars)	Per Project Per Year (in dollars)
HSMHA					
Laboratory research	1	37,640	4.0	37,640	9,410
Laboratory and clinical research	2	371,322	3.5	185,661	53,046
Laboratory, clinical, and epidemiological research	2	771,945	4.0	385,973	96,493
Laboratory and epidemiological research	5	1,392,048	5.8	278,410	48,001
Clinical research	6	986,537	4.7	164,423	35,233
Clinical and epidemiological research	10	2,342,722	5.4	234,272	43,383
Clinical and epidemiological research and student exchange	1	242,362	5.0	242,362	80,787
Epidemiological research	22	8,990,435	4.8	408,656	84,815
Epidemiological research, manpower training, and other	1	718,417	4.0	718,417	179,604
Epidemiological research and other	1	607,500	4.0	607,500	151,875
Conference	9	632,173	1.8	70,241	39,511
Manpower training	3	241,957	3.0	80,652	26,884
Student exchange	3	652,807	6.7	217,602	32,640
Other	4	878,062	4.0	219,515	54,878
HSMHA Totals	70	18,865,927	4.4	269,513	60,857

FDA					
Laboratory research	2	302,263	3.0	151,132	50,377
Laboratory and clinical research	2	350,064	3.5	175,032	50,009
Laboratory and epidemiological research	1	114,715	3.0	114,715	38,238
Clinical and epidemiological research	2	508,734	4.0	254,367	63,591
FDA Totals	7	1,275,776	3.4	182,254	53,157
EPA					
Conference	1	54,000	1.0	54,000	54,000
EPA Totals	1	54,000	1.0	54,000	54,000
Program Totals	110	25,029,105	4.1	227,537	55,009

The least expensive project types in terms of average budget per project were also somewhat unique. Critical reviews were by far the least expensive projects, averaging only $17,510 per project. The eleven conferences had an average budget of some $70,546; and the three manpower-training projects had an average budget of $80,652.

Among the less unusual project types, laboratory research projects had the lowest average total budget per project, some $87,383. The average budgets per project of laboratory and clinical research, $149,145, were also relatively low. On balance, it would seem that laboratory research is a relatively inexpensive undertaking.

The average yearly budgets per project follow the same pattern as the average total budgets. Epidemiological research tends to involve relatively large annual expenditures. Laboratory research tends to involve relatively low annual expenditures.

Although the data in Table 3-10 generally follow the pattern that has been evolving from the data analyzed so far, they do provide certain new insights and suggest certain qualifications to conclusions suggested by the previous data.

The patterns of relative costs of project types are roughly the same within the several agencies as those that were inferred from the overall program data and outlined above. On balance, laboratory research tends to be relatively less expensive and epidemiological research tends to be relatively more expensive within each agency.

HSMHA has in fact spent much more on its Special Foreign Currency Program in Yugoslavia than the other agencies. In part this is due to the absolute size of the HSMHA program in terms of the number of projects supported. But the data in Table 3-10 provide an adequate summary to support the conclusion that HSMHA spends more in part because it tends to support longer projects and projects with larger budgets per year. The average total budget of HSMHA projects is some $269,513, significantly larger than FDA at $182,254, and NIH at $151,044. The average annual budget of HSMHA projects is some $61,253, again larger than FDA at $53,157, and NIH at $39,618. Finally, the average length of HSMHA projects is 4.4 years, while that of FDA is 3.4 years, and that of NIH is 3.5 years.

It has been noted above that NIH tends to concentrate on laboratory research in terms of the number of projects supported. In this respect NIH was differentiated from HSMHA, which tends to support clinical and epidemiological research projects, and FDA, which displays more of a balance of support among all three types. The data in Table 3-10 show the extent to which the number of projects can be a misleading indicator. The total budget to date of the three epidemiological research projects funded by NIH is greater than the total budget to date of all eighteen laboratory research projects. Thus, in spite of the dominance of laboratory research in terms of the number of projects, laboratory research represents only some 30 percent of the NIH program in terms of total budget to date. Even with this qualification, of course, NIH is dominant in the context of laboratory research; that is, NIH has budgeted significantly more for laboratory research than the other agencies separately or combined.

Yugoslav Financial Contributions

Apparently, before this evaluation study was undertaken, there was little or no systematic information available concerning the level of support that Special Foreign Currency Program activities in Yugoslavia received from the host country. The Yugoslav evaluation team was able to provide data on the Yugoslav contribution for 103 of the 110 projects. The pattern of Yugoslav financial support is reflected in the distribution of the Yugoslav contribution as a percent of the U.S. budget to date outlined in Table 3-11.

There was no Yugoslav contribution for twelve of the 103 projects. With one exception, the remaining projects received Yugoslav contributions that ranged between 6 and 18 percent. (The one exception was a HSMHA project with a U.S. budget of \$23,227 that received a Yugoslav contribution of \$12,000, some 52.2 percent.) More than half of all projects received a Yugoslav contribution of 12 to 15 percent. The median Yugoslav contribution was 12.6 percent of the U.S. budget.

There do seem to be some minor differences among the several agencies. All FDA projects received some financial contribution from Yugoslav sources and

Table 3-11

Distribution of Yugoslav Contribution as a Percentage of U.S. Budget to Date by Agency

Yugoslav Contribution (percent)	Number of Projects				
	NIH	HSMHA	FDA	EPA	Total
0	5	6	0	1	12
0.1- 3.0	0	0	0	0	0
3.1- 6.0	0	0	0	0	0
6.1- 9.0	1	1	0	0	2
9.1-12.0	4	16	0	0	20
12.1-15.0	15	34	6	0	55
15.0-18.0	6	6	1	0	13
Over 18	0	1	0	0	1
	31	64	7	1	103
Median Yugoslav contribution (percent)	14.3	12.5	14.8	0.0	12.6

Table 3-12

Summary of U.S. and Yugoslav Financial Support by Type of Research or Major Activity by Agency

Project Type	Number of Projects	U.S. Budget to Date (in dollars)	Yugoslav Financial Contribution (in dollars)	Yugoslav Contribution as a Percent of U.S. Budget to Date
NIH				
Laboratory research	17	1,370,585	195,000	14.2
Laboratory and clinical research	1	23,743	3,000	12.6
Laboratory and epidemiological research	1	56,922	9,000	15.8
Laboratory research and conference	1	279,422	42,000	15.0
Clinical research	1	249,735	37,000	14.8
Clinical and epidemiological research	1	30,741	5,000	16.3
Epidemiological research	3	1,795,442	194,000	10.8
Conference	1	89,833	9,000	10.0
Translations	1	742,378	–	0.0
Critical reviews	4	70,038	–	0.0
NIH Totals	31	4,708,839	494,000	10.5
HSMHA				
Laboratory research	1	37,640	6,000	15.9
Laboratory and clinical research	2	371,322	64,000	17.2
Laboratory, clinical, and epidemiological research	2	771,945	100,000	13.0
Laboratory and epidemiological research	4	591,951	84,000	14.2

Clinical research	6	986,537	148,000	15.0
Clinical and epidemiological research	10	2,342,722	314,000	13.4
Clinical and epidemiological research and student exchange	1	242,362	36,000	14.9
Epidemiological research	20	7,412,122	873,000	11.8
Epidemiological research and other	1	607,500	76,000	12.5
Conference	7	586,917	3,000	5.0
Manpower training	3	241,957	25,000	10.3
Student exchange	3	652,807	65,000	10.0
Other	4	878,062	112,000	12.8
HSMHA Totals	64	15,723,844	1,906,000	12.1
FDA				
Laboratory research	2	302,263	45,000	14.8
Laboratory and clinical research	2	350,064	52,000	14.9
Laboratory and epidemiological research	1	114,715	17,000	14.8
Clinical and epidemiological research	2	508,734	70,000	13.8
FDA Totals	7	1,275,776	184,000	14.4
EPA				
Conference	1	54,000	–	0.0
EPA Totals	1	54,000	–	0.0
Program Totals	103	21,762,459	2,584,000	11.9

the median Yugoslav contribution to FDA projects was higher than those to the projects of the other agencies. NIH had proportionately more projects that received no Yugoslav contribution, but the median Yugoslav contribution to NIH projects was somewhat higher than that to HSMHA projects.

The data in Table 3-12 represent a summary of the U.S. and Yugoslav financial support of the program by type of research or major activity outlined by agency. The translation project and the four critical review projects were those among the NIH program that did not receive a Yugoslav contribution. Six of the seven conferences were those among the HSMHA program that did not receive a Yugoslav contribution.

Among the NIH project types that received some level of Yugoslav financial support, the conference and the epidemiological research project types received proportionately less support than others. Among the HSMHA project types, conferences clearly received proportionately less support than others.

There is a limit to what can reasonably be inferred from these data, but they may imply something about Yugoslav priorities.

Gauging Domestic Yugoslav Health Objectives

The assessment of the impact of the Special Foreign Currency Program in Yugoslavia was primarily the responsibility of the Yugoslav team. The question of health objectives and priorities in Yugoslavia concerned their evaluation team in the same sense that the Harvard team faced the issue in assessing the impact of the program on the achievement of U.S. domestic health objectives.

The Yugoslav team developed a list of Yugoslav health objectives. This list is outlined in Table 3-13.

The major efforts of the two evaluation teams to assess the impact of the Special Foreign Currency Program in the two countries is the subject of the rest of this volume.

Table 3-13
Domestic Health Objectives of Yugoslavia

1. Efficiency in health services delivery
   Economy in health
   Use of manpower and equipment/facilities/in health
   Planning and programming in health services

2. Education and improvement of manpower in health

3. The effect of biological active substances

4. Population and family planning
   Reproduction control and investigation
   Social and medical demography
   Factors influencing fertility regulation
   Public health aspects of family planning

5. Promotion of preventive health care

6. Control and prevention of disability and invalidity

7. Environmental protection
   Air pollution
   Noise
   Water
   Waste materials
   Pesticides
   Ionizing raying

8. Epidemiology of chronic noninfectious diseases

9. Reduction of morbidity and mortality

10. Influence of industrialization, urbanization, and other social factors on health

11. Promotion of positive health life
    Nutrition
    Growth and development
    Health education

12. Investigation in geriatric field/geriatry

13. Social welfare and juvenile delinquency

14. Experimental biological/medical/investigation

15. Promotion of medical information and health statistics

4

An Evaluation of the Special Foreign Currency Program in Yugoslavia

Introduction

The objective of this study was to assess the impact of the Special Foreign Currency Program on the United States and Yugoslavia. The primary technique for gathering data relevant to the impact of projects involved a standard questionnaire for project review answered by the members of the two evaluation teams. The questionnaire was designed to provide information concerning relative progress, cooperative efforts, project impact, and other relevant information. A copy of the Questionnaire for Project Review is included in the Appendix (p.153).

Between the two evaluation teams there are actually three sets of responses. One member of the Harvard evaluation team was responsible for reviewing all 110 projects and answering the standard questionnaire for each. Thus, one set of responses is available from a single individual reviewer. The remaining members of the Harvard team were responsible for reviewing certain of the projects and answering the standard questionnaire for those. In most cases the individual projects were reviewed by that member of the team whose expertise was most relevant to the particular type of research or major activity of the project. Hence, a second set of responses is available from the Harvard team. Approximately 10 percent of the projects were reviewed at team meetings in order to promote a maximum feasible consistency among the reviews.

The Yugoslav team employed a somewhat different approach. Each member of the team was assigned a number of projects to review on the basis of his particular competence and the area of concern of the specific projects. The individual reviewer was responsible for gathering all information relevant to the project and for presenting his general assessment to the entire team. When it came to answering the standard questionnaire, however, the final judgments represented a team consensus.

Among the three sets of responses there may be varying degrees of consistency to the 110 reviews. Presumably the single reviewer should be most consistent in his interpretation of questions, for example. The several reviewers answering more or less independently would be expected to display the least consistency. In any event, the three sets of responses are available for analysis, and a significant byproduct of this study may be derived from determining whether the approach to assessing the kinds of information involved in this evaluation makes a significant difference in the outcome.

Analysis of the Questionnaire Responses

The most straightforward way to summarize the responses to the questionnaire is to simply present answers to representative relevant questions. A number of general comments may facilitate the interpretation of these answers.

First, there are three sets of responses. The single reviewer from the Harvard team is classified as "S," the set of responses from the other Harvard reviewers is classified as "H," and the set of responses from the Yugoslav team is classified as "Y."

Second, the data base for these sets of responses were the 100 projects started between 1960 and 1972. The responses of the single reviewer, S, will always sum to 110. The H responses will sum to 112, due to the fact that two projects were reviewed twice by the other Harvard reviewers. The Y responses will sum to 111, since one project was reviewed twice by the Yugoslav team.

Third, for many questions "not known" and "not applicable" were possible answers. It was intended that these answers would be offered most sparingly, but may have been used more often than was appropriate. In order to cope with this problem, and in some cases in order to facilitate comparisons among the different reviewers, the mean response is often calculated in two ways: (1) The not-known and not-applicable answers are ignored and the mean response calculated for the remaining responses; and (2) the not-known and not-ap-plicable answers are treated as if they were "no" benefit, "no" contribution, "no" impact, etc. These will be referred to as "Mean (1)" and "Mean (2)."

Fourth, in certain cases the American and Yugoslav reviewers were answering different questions. This was the case whenever the two teams by agreement interpreted questions for their specific countries. In these instances, of course, the responses are not strictly comparable, and this will be indicated.

Fifth, the Special Foreign Currency Program in Yugoslavia in fact is overwhelmingly a recent program. Of the 110 projects reviewed, 95 were not scheduled to be completed by the end of 1971. Further, of the fifteen projects scheduled to end by 1971, many were so recent that they had not yet attained publication, while other publications had not had the time to achieve near full impact. Consequently the several reviewers had to make projections of potential impact rather than attempt to assess actual impact in the vast majority of cases. The sections on project impact in this chapter should, therefore, be interpreted essentially in terms of potential impact. There is a section in Chapter 5 that deals with actual impact where it could be analyzed for a relatively small number of projects.

Sixth, the subjective nature of these reviews should be kept in mind. There are, unfortunately, no universally accepted standards for measuring the effects upon a health care system or for gauging the results of health-related research. An attempt has been made to obtain standards by asking a large group of competent consultants to read carefully through a large number of research projects and to answer a long series of difficult, judgmental question. The answers to these questions were couched in what might be referred to as "semi-quantitative terms." It is clear that there is a significant subjective latitude in the understanding of these terms. Every effort should be made in interpreting the response data to remain aware of these inevitable sources of uncertainty. Whenever reasonable doubt exists that an inference upon the impact of the projects might be due to different subjective interpretations, it is perhaps better to reserve judgment than to draw the inference.

Finally, the main conclusions that can be drawn from the responses are summative in nature. Thus, for example, the reviewers rated the proposed project benefits in relation to the budget allocated as slightly less than great. That is, the mean response of 2.12 lies between the answers "2. Great benefit" and "3. Some benefit." Such summative estimations are presented for all of the questions answered and provide the basis for limited statements about the directions of the impact of the program. For example, the impact on Yugoslavia was judged to be higher upon its scientific establishment than upon its health care system. Yet there is a basic problem of interpretation. Simply because the answers to the two questions are couched in the same language does not necessarily mean that the more important effects were felt in the scientific establishment. A "small" contribution to the health care system may in fact be as valuable as "some" contribution to the scientific establishment.

Specific Advantage of Yugoslavia

The reviewers were asked to rate the significance of the specific advantages of implementing the project in Yugoslavia rather than in the United States. The responses:

	S	H	Y	Total
1. Maximal advantage	15	15	5	35
2. Great advantage	55	35	45	135
3. Some advantage	32	19	46	97
4. Small advantage	1	29	11	41
5. No advantage	0	12	2	14
6. Not known	0	0	0	0
7. Not applicable	5	2	2	9
No answer	2	0	0	2
	110	112	111	333
Mean (1)	2.18	2.89	2.63	2.58
Mean (2)	2.31	2.93	2.68	2.64

In terms of whether or not the specific projects could be implemented in Yugoslavia to some advantage over implementing them in the United States, the

Special Foreign Currency Program appears to do well. There are a number of projects that in the view of the several reviewers could be implemented in Yugoslavia to maximal advantage over implementing them in the United States. The single Harvard reviewer rates no fewer than fifteen projects in this category, and the other Harvard reviewers rate fifteen projects in this category. Even if one were to assume that they were the same fifteen projects, the minimum number of projects for which implementation in Yugoslavia was considered to be a maximal advantage to at least one Harvard reviewer was fifteen. The Yugoslav reviewers rated only five projects in the maximal advantage category. Further, for a significant number of projects, the several reviewers rated the significance of the specific advantages of implementing the project in Yugoslavia rather than in the United States as great. Finally, the mean responses of all reviewers lies between some advantage and great advantage, and serves as a summary statistic representing the specific advantage of Yugoslavia for projects funded under the program.

Relative Progress of the Projects

A number of questions were asked that were related to the relative progress of projects. The first of these questions simply asked whether or not the reviewer felt that reasonable progress had been made in terms of the original time schedule of the project. The responses:

	S	H	Y	Total
Yes	75	74	104	253
No	13	9	7	29
No answer	22	29	0	51
	110	112	111	333

The interpretation of what constitutes reasonable progress is clearly not the same among the several reviewers.

The second question asked whether or not significant cost overruns had been incurred. The responses:

	S	H	Y	Total
Yes	32	32	12	76
No	78	80	96	254
No answer	0	0	3	3
	110	112	111	333

In fact, the Harvard team did eventually develop a criterion for identifying cost overruns. A project was classified as having incurred a significant cost overrun if its budget was increased by more than 50 percent or more than $50,000. Thirty-two projects did have significant cost overruns by this criterion.

The reviewers were asked to rate the proposed project objectives in relation to the budget allocated. The responses:

	S	H	Y	Total
1. Maximal benefit	31	12	10	53
2. Great benefit	56	59	82	197
3. Some benefit	19	31	18	68
4. Small benefit	2	9	1	12
5. No benefit	0	0	0	0
6. Not known	0	0	0	0
7. Not applicable	0	0	0	0
No answer	2	1	0	3
	110	112	111	333
Mean	1.93	2.33	2.09	2.12

In the case of each reviewer, a significant number of projects were rated as having maximal or great benefits in relation to the budget allocated. On balance, the reviewers rated the proposed project benefits in relation to budget as slightly less than great, as implied by the total mean response of 2.12. They were also asked to rate the actual project accomplishments in relation to the budget allocated. The responses:

	S	H	Y	Total
1. Maximal benefit	6	9	14	29
2. Great benefit	25	28	67	120
3. Some benefit	23	22	27	72
4. Small benefit	3	14	2	19
5. No benefit	0	1	1	2
6. Not known	48	22	0	70
7. Not applicable	1	12	0	13
No answer	4	4	0	8
	110	112	111	333
Mean (1)	2.40	2.59	2.18	2.36
Mean (2)	3.60	3.35	2.18	3.03

In the case of each set of responses, actual accomplishments were ranked somewhat lower than proposed objectives. This might be due to a number of factors, and perhaps no definitive conclusion would be appropriate. It may be that a comparison of these two sets of responses reflects the lack of reasonable progress for some projects, however.

The Relative Importance of the Projects

The reviewers were asked to rate the relative importance for both Yugoslavia and the United States of the diseases, disorders, or conditions studied. The responses for Yugoslavia:

	S	H	Y	Total
1. Most important	0	7	7	14
2. Very important	27	30	40	97
3. Important	53	39	49	141
4. Not very important	11	13	6	30
5. Not important	1	1	0	2
6. Not known	0	1	0	1
7. Not applicable	16	21	9	46
No answer	2	0	0	2
	110	112	111	333
Mean (1)	2.85	2.68	2.53	2.68
Mean (2)	3.17	3.13	2.73	3.01

The responses for the United States:

	S	H	Y	Total
1. Most important	2	5	3	10
2. Very important	23	26	22	71
3. Important	52	32	53	137
4. Not very important	11	19	12	42
5. Not important	4	4	0	8
6. Not known	0	1	11	12
7. Not applicable	16	24	10	50
No answer	2	1	0	3
	110	112	111	333
Mean (1)	2.91	2.90	2.82	2.88
Mean (2)	3.22	3.37	3.23	3.28

The responses tend to cluster in the important and very important categories, with some not very important and some not applicable. On balance, the reviewers rated the diseases, disorders, or conditions studied slightly more than important for the United States and somewhat more important for Yugoslavia. Thus, the projects do tend to deal with important problems, but not with those of highest priority in either country.

Comparable Research Projects

The reviewers were asked to identify comparable research projects and to compare the Special Foreign Currency Program in Yugoslavia under review with any comparable research projects known to them. The responses:

	S	H	Y	Total
1. Very much better	0	3	3	6
2. Somewhat better	0	5	11	16
3. About the same	9	16	22	47
4. Not quite as good	0	4	1	5
5. Much worse	0	1	0	1
6. Not known	15	30	0	45
7. Not applicable	83	37	74	194
No answer	3	16	0	19
	110	112	111	333
Mean (1)	3.00	2.83	2.57	2.72

Any conclusions drawn from these responses must first take note of the fact that the majority of responses were either not known or not applicable. These responses apparently reflect the fact that in the majority of cases the reviewer was not personally aware of any comparable research projects. However, the reviewers did rate the projects of the Special Foreign Currency Program in Yugoslavia as slightly better than comparable research projects known to them. Since it seems reasonable to speculate that the different reviewers were more likely to be familiar with comparable projects in their own country, the Yugoslav response may indicate that the Special Foreign Currency Program involves some of that country's better researchers. In the same context, the American responses of not known and not applicable are perhaps quite consistent with the conclusion suggested above that there is a significant specific advantage to implementing certain projects, perhaps even project types, in Yugoslavia.

Cooperative Efforts

The reviewers were asked to rank the nonfinancial contributions of the United States in the form of such contributions as manpower, scientific guidance, and methodological support. Their responses:

	S	H	Y	Total
1. Maximal contribution	2	2	2	6
2. Great contribution	23	38	42	103
3. Some contribution	34	30	54	118
4. Small contribution	24	25	12	61
5. No contribution	20	14	0	34
6. Not known	4	3	1	8
7. Not applicable	1	0	0	1
No answer	2	0	0	2
	110	112	111	333
Mean (1)	3.36	3.10	2.69	3.04
Mean (2)	3.44	3.15	2.71	3.10

The American reviewers ranked the U.S. nonfinancial contributions somewhat lower than the Yugoslavs did.

The extent of any contributions by parties other than the United States and Yugoslavia was also rated. The rankings were:

	S	H	Y	Total
1. Maximal contribution	0	1	0	1
2. Great contribution	9	12	10	31
3. Some contribution	16	16	13	45
4. Small contribution	4	6	8	18
5. No contribution	67	69	78	214
6. Not known	11	7	2	20
7. Not applicable	1	0	0	1
No answer	2	1	0	3
	110	112	111	333
Mean (1)	4.34	4.25	4.41	4.34

Albeit there were a few projects that received significant contributions from third parties, the majority of projects received none and the extent of contributions to the program by parties other than the U.S. and Yugoslavia was rated less than small by all the reviewers.

Project Impact

A number of questions were included to gauge the general impact of the projects reviewed. In each case the reviewers were asked to assess the actual impact for completed projects or the potential impact for uncompleted projects. The first of these questions asked for the reviewer's assessment of the contribution to the Yugoslav scientific establishment. The responses were:

	S	H	Y	Total
1. Maximal contribution	2	5	6	13
2. Great contribution	4	27	30	61
3. Some contribution	28	37	57	122
4. Small contribution	42	27	15	84
5. No contribution	30	14	0	44
6. Not known	1	1	0	2
7. Not applicable	1	1	3	5
No answer	2	0	0	2
	110	112	111	333
Mean (1)	3.89	3.16	2.75	3.26
Mean (2)	3.91	3.20	2.81	3.30

The reviewers were also asked to assess the contribution to the U.S. scientific establishment. The responses were:

	S	H	Y	Total
1. Maximal contribution	0	1	0	1
2. Great contribution	0	16	5	21
3. Some contribution	1	32	41	74
4. Small contribution	10	27	24	61
5. No contribution	94	32	3	129
6. Not known	0	3	33	36
7. Not applicable	3	1	5	9
No answer	2	0	0	2
	110	112	111	333
Mean (1)	4.89	3.68	3.34	4.03
Mean (2)	4.89	3.72	3.91	4.17

In addition, the reviewers were asked to assess the contributions to the Yugoslav health care system and the U.S. health care system respectively. For the Yugoslav health care system the responses were:

	S	H	Y	Total
1. Maximal contribution	2	5	6	13
2. Great contribution	4	27	30	61
3. Some contribution	28	37	57	122
4. Small contribution	42	27	15	84
5. No contribution	30	14	0	44
6. Not known	1	1	0	2
7. Not applicable	1	1	3	5
No answer	2	0	0	2
	110	112	111	333
Mean (1)	4.22	3.78	2.96	3.64
Mean (2)	4.31	3.83	3.07	3.73

For the U.S. health care system the responses were:

	S	H	Y	Total
1. Maximal contribution	0	0	1	1
2. Great contribution	3	12	10	25
3. Some contribution	8	20	14	42
4. Small contribution	9	30	15	54
5. No contribution	79	45	8	132
6. Not known	0	2	59	61
7. Not applicable	8	3	4	15
No answer	3	0	0	3
	110	112	111	333
Mean (1)	4.66	4.01	3.40	4.15
Mean (2)	4.68	4.05	4.31	4.34

In all four cases the American reviewers assessed the impact to be somewhat lower than did the Yugoslav reviewers. In general, the impact on the scientific establishment was considered to be somewhat greater than the impact on the health care system for each country. Finally, the impact was generally considered to be somewhat less in the United States than it was in Yugoslavia.

These several characteristics are perhaps related. In any event, the assessments of the reviewers undoubtedly represent a complex set of considerations. If the impact in general is in fact higher in Yugoslavia than it is in the United States, it might be expected that the Yugoslav reviewers would assess impact to be somewhat higher in any specific context. Favorable experience does after all contribute to favorable expectations.

The nature of the Special Foreign Currency Program is such that one would expect that the impact on the scientific establishment of Yugoslavia would be somewhat more than the impact on the scientific establishment of the United States. The apparent pessimism implicit in the general tendency of the Harvard reviewers to assess the impact on the two health care systems as small or near small is also understandable. A number of factors might have contributed to this general assessment. First, of course, most of the projects were not complete, and the reviewers were assessing potential impact and perhaps appropriately discounting for uncertainty. Second, the nature of much health-related research is such that there is often a rather significant time lag between the research and the eventual impact on health, per se. Finally, of course, many specific research findings may have a significant impact on a particular disease or treatment modality but not really affect the health care *system*. (On this point it should be noted that an attempt was made to impress upon all reviewers that the question be interpreted with the emphasis on the word "system." That is, the concern was with the actual or potential for contributions that would have an impact on the delivery system per se. Given the actual distribution of the responses, it seems reasonable to conclude that the several reviewers did not interpret this question the same way.)

The reviewers were asked to rate the contributions of the projects to medical knowledge or other health-related knowledge. The responses were:

	S	H	Y	Total
1. Maximal contribution	0	0	1	1
2. Great contribution	9	31	22	62
3. Some contribution	45	43	76	164
4. Small contribution	31	26	6	63
5. No contribution	19	8	0	27
6. Not known	2	3	1	6
7. Not applicable	2	1	5	8
No answer	2	0	0	2
	110	112	111	333
Mean (1)	3.58	3.10	2.83	3.17
Mean (2)	3.63	3.17	2.95	3.24

These responses seem consistent with those concerning the contributions to the scientific establishment. The Yugoslav reviewers assess the contributions to knowledge somewhat higher, but the American reviewers certainly rate the contributions to be more than small.

In a related question the reviewers were asked to rate the contributions in terms of stimulating further research. The responses were:

	S	H	Y	Total
1. Maximal contribution	2	4	3	9
2. Great contribution	10	24	42	76
3. Some contribution	65	37	54	156
4. Small contribution	23	30	9	62
5. No contribution	6	11	0	17
6. Not known	1	3	0	4
7. Not applicable	1	3	3	7
No answer	2	0	0	2
	110	112	111	333
Mean (1)	3.20	3.19	2.64	3.01
Mean (2)	3.23	3.29	2.70	3.07

The same general pattern of responses prevails for contributions in terms of the stimulation of further research as did for contributions to knowledge. The contributions are clearly considered to be more than small by all reviewers, and more than some by the Yugoslav reviewers.

Impact on U.S. Domestic Health Objectives

In order to assess the impact of the Special Foreign Currency Program in Yugoslavia on the U.S. domestic health objectives, the American reviewers were asked to rate the actual contribution for completed projects or the potential contribution of uncompleted projects to each of the ten domestic health objectives discussed and outlined in Chapter 2. A summary of their responses is outlined in Tables 4-1 and 4-2.

These data must be interpreted with great care. First, of course, the overwhelming majority of the responses are for uncompleted projects. Hence, the relevant context is most often potential contribution. In order to reflect this fact, the discussion in this section of the impact of the Special Foreign Currency Program on the U.S. domestic health objectives is couched in terms of potential contribution.

Second, the fact that these responses represent subjective data should be kept in mind. Even when actual impact is the issue, the response is not an objective measurement, but rather a subjective assessment. The assessment of potential contribution is a particularly complex task. At the very least, it is more complicated by the need to assess subjective probabilities of success.

Table 4-1
Summary of the Single Harvard Reviewer's Assessment of the Actual or Potential Contribution to U.S. Domestic Health Objectives of the Special Foreign Currency Program in Yugoslavia

Objectives	Contribution						Not Applicable	No Answer	Total	Mean (1)
	Maximal	Great	Some	Small	None	Not Known				
Curing diseases	0	2	16	17	47	1	25	2	110	4.33
Morbidity reduction	0	4	18	13	47	1	25	2	110	4.26
Preventive health care advances	0	3	13	14	55	0	23	2	110	4.42
Promote positive health life	0	0	11	8	65	0	24	2	110	4.64
Improved geriatric care	0	0	5	5	73	0	25	2	110	4.82
Improved treatment of mental disorders	0	0	5	3	76	1	23	2	110	4.85
Efficient health services delivery	0	4	10	5	69	0	20	2	110	4.58
Equitable and efficient costing arrangements	0	0	0	0	82	0	26	2	110	5.00
Solutions to environmental problems	0	0	8	2	76	0	22	2	110	4.79
Improved health information	0	1	13	15	62	0	17	2	110	4.52
	0	14	99	82	652	3	230	20	1100	4.62

Table 4-2
Summary of the Other Harvard Reviewers' Assessment of the Actual or Potential Contribution to U.S. Domestic Health Objectives of the Special Foreign Currency Program in Yugoslavia

Objectives	Contribution								Total	Mean (1)
	Maximal	Great	Some	Small	None	Not Known	Not Applicable	No Answer		
Curing diseases	1	7	14	27	46	6	11	0	112	4.16
Morbidity reduction	0	14	17	32	37	7	5	0	112	3.92
Preventive health care advances	0	21	21	32	31	7	0	0	112	3.70
Promote positive health life	0	9	16	14	60	9	4	0	112	4.26
Improved geriatric care	1	3	10	13	70	6	8	1	112	4.53
Improved treatment of mental disorders	0	4	7	15	72	4	10	0	112	4.58
Efficient health services delivery	0	11	16	15	62	2	6	0	112	4.23
Equitable and efficient costing arrangements	0	1	5	5	82	7	12	0	112	4.81
Solutions to environmental problems	4	13	17	12	51	5	10	0	112	3.96
Improved health information	3	17	39	22	25	5	1	0	112	3.46
	9	100	162	187	536	58	67	1	1120	4.15

Finally, the nature and meaning of the given responses, whether actual or potential, must be carefully interpreted if they are to provide a relevant and useful perspective of the program. It would be inappropriate, for example, to simply calculate the mean responses for the ten objectives and use them to draw the conclusion that the potential contribution of the program to the U.S. domestic health objectives was quite small. In order to appreciate this one need only consider the following hypothetical set of circumstances. Suppose a hypothetical program was established and designed to fund one hundred projects such that ten projects were to concentrate exclusively on each of the ten health objectives with a goal of each project making a maximal contribution to the health objective it was concerned with. Suppose further that the goal was achieved for each project, and that there were no indirect effects on health objectives other than the one with which each project was concerned. What would a review of this hypothetical program generate for a set of responses? Each project would be assessed as having made a maximal contribution to one of the ten health objectives and no contribution to the other nine. The mean response for each health objective would be 4.6 (10 x 1 + 90 x 5/100). Clearly the number of projects that make a significant contribution to at least one health objective is more relevant for assessing the program than are the mean contributions of all projects to all health objectives.

On the other hand it would be equally inappropriate to treat the raw sum of responses of significant contribution as evidence that the potential contribution of the program to the U.S. domestic health objectives was quite high. Again an extreme but simple example should make the point. Suppose the hypothetical program of one hundred projects included ten that made a maximal contribution to all ten health objectives and ninety that made no contribution to any of them. What would a review of this hypothetical program generate for a set of responses? Ten projects would be assessed as having made a maximal contribution to each of the ten health objectives, so the raw sum of maximal contributions would be one hundred. Again, the number of projects that make a significant contribution to at least one health objective is more relevant to an assessment of the program than is the raw sum of responses of significant contribution.

Finally, albeit the number of projects that make a significant contribution to at least one health objective is relevant to an assessment of the program, it does not necessarily give a complete indication of the impact of the program on the domestic health objectives. Since some projects may in fact make contributions to more than one health objective, some indication of the number of projects making multiple contributions is relevant to an assessment of the impact of the program.

The data in Tables 4-3 and 4-4 provide the additional information necessary to make a more appropriate assessment of the impact of the program on the U.S. domestic health objectives. Table 4-3 includes a breakdown of the number of

Table 4-3

Number of Projects with Actual or Potential Contributions to at Least One U.S. Domestic Health Objective by Level of Highest Contribution as Assessed by Harvard Reviewers

Level of Contribution	Number of Projects	
	S	H
Maximal	0	7
Great	10	38
Some	52	34
Small	27	23
None	12	5
Not known	0	3
Not applicable	7	0
No answer	2	0
	110	110

projects with potential contributions to at least one U.S. domestic health objective by the level of the highest potential contribution, as assessed by the Harvard reviewers. Thus, for example, the single Harvard reviewer considered

Table 4-4

Summary of the Number of Projects by the Number of U.S. Domestic Health Objectives for Which They Have Potential Contributions

Number of Domestic Health Objectives Contributed to	Number of Projects with					
	Maximal or Great Contribution		Maximal, Great or Some Contribution		Any Contribution	
	S	H	S	H	S	H
0	100	65	48	32	21	9
1	8	13	36	17	36	13
2	1	15	14	7	27	5
3	–	10	4	16	11	18
4	1	1	5	15	9	16
5	–	5	2	12	1	15
6	–	1	1	9	5	14
7	–	–	–	1	–	11
8	–	–	–	–	–	6
9	–	–	–	–	–	1
10	–	–	–	1	–	2
	110	110	110	110	110	110

none of the 110 projects to have the potential for a maximal contribution to any domestic health objective. In his assessment, 10 projects have the potential for a great contribution to at least one health objective, 52 have the potential for some contribution to at least one health objective, and 27 have the potential for a small contribution to at least one health objective. The other Harvard reviewers tend to rate the projects somewhat more favorably, considering 7 to have the potential for a maximal contribution to at least one domestic health objective, 38 to have the potential for a great contribution to at least one health objective, and so forth.

Table 4-4 provides a further breakdown of the data in the form of a summary of the number of projects by the actual number of U.S. domestic health objectives to which they may make contributions of varying levels. These data provide the perspective on multiple contributions necessary to make a more complete assessment of the impact of the program. The interpretation of the data in this table is rather straightforward. Thus, for example, in the assessment of the single Harvard reviewer eight projects have the potential for a great contribution to one domestic health objective, one project has the potential for a great contribution to two domestic health objectives, and one project has the potential for a great contribution to four domestic health objectives. (If the reader does not recognize these as the ten projects with a great contribution to at least one domestic health objective listed in Table 4-3 and the fourteen responses of great contribution summarized in Table 4-1, then the interpretation is not as straightforward as claimed.) Further, by his assessment, one hundred projects did not have the potential for a maximal or great contribution to any domestic health objective. As before, the other Harvard reviewers tend to rate the projects somewhat more favorably, considering only 65 to have no potential for a maximal or great contribution to any domestic health objective while assessing 13 to have a potential for a maximal or great contribution to one domestic health objective, 15 to have a potential for a maximal or great contribution to two domestic health objectives, 10 to have such a potential for contribution to three health objectives, and so forth.[a]

A careful consideration of the information available in Tables 4-1 through 4-4 can provide a reasonable indication of the potential impact of the Special Foreign Currency Program in Yugoslavia on the U.S. domestic health objectives. First, the data in Tables 4-1 and 4-2 provide some perspective of the relative potential impact of the program on the ten objectives. In the assessment of the single Harvard reviewer significant (maximal or great) potential contributions can be made to only five domestic health objectives by the program. (For

---

[a]These are the 7 projects with a maximal contribution to at least one domestic health objective plus the 38 projects with a great contribution to at least one domestic health objective listed in Table 4-3. They represent only 108 of the 109 responses of maximal or great contribution summarized in Table 4-2 because the two extra reviews have been eliminated from these data to avoid double counting.

convenience, in the discussion that follows maximal and great are combined and referred to as significant.) The other Harvard reviewers have rated the projects more favorably in terms of their potential contributions and credit the program with significant potential contributions to all of the ten objectives. Even though the two assessments are different in terms of absolute magnitudes, there does appear to be a pattern of consistency in terms of the potential impact of the program on the several objectives at the significant contribution level. A comparison of the five objectives to which significant contributions are likely in the opinion of the single reviewer and the five objectives which rank highest among the other reviewers in terms of significant contributions, reflects four that are common to both—Preventive Health Care Advances, Improved Health Information, Morbidity Reduction, and Efficient Health Services Delivery. The single reviewer credits the program with somewhat more potential impact on Curing Diseases and considerably less potential impact on Solutions to Environmental Problems.

When the assessments of some potential contribution to the ten objectives are added the pattern of consistency in terms of the potential impact of the program is even more pronounced. The relative ranks of the ten objecives remain the same for the other Harvard reviewers, and the original five objectives are ranked as the first five by the single Harvard reviewer. The same four objectives remain common to the five ranked highest by each. Finally, both the single Harvard reviewer and the other Harvard reviewers have the same U.S. domestic health objectives ranked lowest in terms of potential impact. The program has the least likely impact on the objectives of Improved Geriatric Care, Improved Treatment of Mental Disorders, and Equitable and Efficient Costing Arrangements.

When the assessments of any potential contribution to the objectives are added the pattern remains essentially the same. On balance, the potential impact of the program on the ten domestic health objectives is as outlined in Table 4-5. The program has more potential for impact on the U.S. domestic objectives such as Improved Health Information, Preventive Health Care Advances, Morbidity Reduction, and Curing Diseases. The program has less potential for impact on the objectives of Improved Geriatric Care, Improved Treatment of Mental Disorders, and Equitable and Efficient Costing Arrangements.

While the data in Tables 4-1 and 4-2 provide an indication of which domestic health objectives are more likely to be affected by the Special Foreign Currency Program in Yugoslavia and which are less likely to be affected, the data in Tables 4-3 and 4-4 provide the information necessary to assess the extent of the potential impact. An indication of the number of projects with the potential for contributing to at least one U.S. domestic health objective is available from Table 4-3. These data allow for an assessment of the program in terms of the proportion of the projects which have the potential for impact. The single Harvard reviewer considers 10 of the projects to have the potential for great contribution, 52 to have the potential for some contribution, and 27 to have the

Table 4-5

Summary of the Potential Impact of the Special Foreign Currency Program in Yugoslavia on the U.S. Domestic Health Objectives

	Objectives in Order of Potential Impact of SFCP in Yugoslavia		
Rank	S	H	Consensus
1	Morbidity reduction	Improved health information	Improved health information
2	Curing diseases	Preventive health care advances	Preventive health care advances
3	Preventive health care advances	Morbidity reduction	Morbidity reduction
4	Improved health information	Solution to environmental problems	Curing diseases
5	Efficient health services delivery	Curing diseases	Solutions to environmental problems
6	Promote positive health life	Efficient health services delivery	Efficient health services delivery
7	Solutions to environmental problems	Promote positive health life	Promote positive health life
8	Improved geriatric care	Improved geriatric care	Improved geriatric care
9	Improved treatment of mental disorders	Improved treatment of mental disorders	Improved treatment of mental disorders
10	Equitable and efficient costing arrangements	Equitable and efficient costing arrangements	Equitable and efficient costing arrangements

potential for small contribution to at least one U.S. domestic health objective. By his assessment, therefore, 81 percent of the projects are expected to make at least a small contribution to the U.S. domestic health objectives, 56 percent are expected to make at least some contribution, and 9 percent are expected to make a significant contribution.

The other Harvard reviewers consider 7, 38, 34, and 23 of the projects to have the potential for maximal, great, some, and small contributions, respectively, to at least one of the U.S. domestic health objectives. Hence, by their assessment, 93 percent of the projects are expected to make at least a small contribution to the U.S. domestic health objectives, 72 percent of the projects are expected to make at least some contribution, and 41 percent are expected to make a significant contribution.

Finally, the data in Table 4-4 provide the perspective on multiple contributions necessary for a more complete assessment of the potential impact of the program. According to the assessment of the single Harvard reviewer, there does appear to be a moderate multiple contribution dimension to the Special Foreign

Currency Program. However, the general pattern of the program reflected in his responses is one of projects that characteristically contribute to a small number of U.S. domestic health objectives. At each level of contribution he rates the majority of projects as contributing to one or two U.S. domestic health objectives. By contrast, the program would appear to be characterized by an extreme dimension of multiple contribution from the responses of the other Harvard reviewers.

A significant difference between the responses of the single Harvard reviewer and the other Harvard reviewers has been apparent throughout this section. The other reviewers have consistently rated the projects more favorably. The difference is particularly pronounced in terms of the multiple contributions to several domestic health objectives by individual projects. (Actually, however, it should be noted that similar differences exist among the responses of the nine individual reviewers who collectively make up the other Harvard reviewers. In fact, two of the nine other reviewers generally rate the projects somewhat less favorably than the single reviewer does.)

There are several factors that might account for the apparent differences. Perhaps the most obvious is the subjective nature of these responses. Different individuals may have quite different opinions of what constitutes a contribution and, more significant perhaps, how important a particular contribution is within a given context.

Since the majority of the responses involved potential contributions, there may be real differences in the process of assessing potential impact. It is quite possible that the single Harvard reviewer assesses the probability of success to be somewhat lower generally than do the other reviewers. He could even have a keener appreciation of the appropriateness of accounting for subjective probabilities of success in assessing potential impact than his colleagues.

There may simply be a difference in the way the single reviewer and the other reviewers interpret specific answers. That is, they might agree on what constitutes a contribution, the relative importance of the contribution in some general sense, and the probability of that contribution actually coming about, and then simply record a different response. There is some indication that there may be such a difference in interpretation of answers. A comparison of the respective summaries of responses in Tables 4-1 and 4-2 reflects a distinct similarity between the single reviewer's responses of great and some and the other reviewers' responses of maximal and great. He records no maximal responses, but has 14 great and 99 some responses; they record 9 maximal and 100 great responses. It is a distinct possibility that much of the apparent difference in the two assessments of the impact of the program derives from different connotations applicable to the words "maximal," "great," and "some." This would imply a semantic difference, but not a real difference in their responses.

Finally, a particular problem of general interpretation might have contributed to the apparent differences in their assessments of the impact of the program.

During the joint reviews at team meetings a number of individual reviewers expressed concern when good projects were rated as having no contribution to make to most of the ten U.S. domestic health objectives. They seemed to feel that a good project rated with a large number of no contributions would appear to be a poor project in the summary statistics. In effect, it is possible that the reviewers had the notion that the mean response would be the criterion for drawing conclusions about the potential contribution of the program to the U.S. domestic health objectives. (Actually their concern was, as stated, that a good project would not appear good if it had a low mean response, but the effect is the same.) This is the criterion that was described above as inappropriate.

There is some indication that many reviewers, including the single reviewer, introduced some bias into their responses in a well-intentioned attempt to rank good projects in such a way that they would be "recognized" as good projects. Again a comparison of the respective summaries of responses in Tables 4-1 and 4-2 may provide some insight into this particular phenomenon. The single reviewer has recorded some 230 responses of not applicable. Presumably he intends those responses to indicate that the research or other activity of the project was not applicable to specific U.S. domestic health objectives. But if the project was not applicable to a specific objective it presumably had no contribution to make to that objective. He apparently felt more comfortable with the illusion that not applicable was in some sense less damning than no contribution; indeed, after the fact he concurred with this general explanation of the phenomenon. The single reviewer recorded not applicable almost three and one-half times as often as did the other reviewers.

On the other hand, the other reviewers recorded a response of small contribution more than twice as often as the single reviewer did. It is quite possible that they were employing the response of small contribution in much the way and for the same purpose as he was employing the response of not applicable. To the extent that this was the case, the apparent difference between the two sets of responses takes on new meaning. If in fact the other reviewers were recording small contribution when the single reviewer was recording not applicable, it is conceivable that they would record some contribution when he recorded small contribution.

On balance, it would appear that the relevant comparison between the two sets of responses is the relative responses rather than the absolute responses. The relative responses were quite consistent and provide approximately the same general assessment of the potential impact of the program on the U.S. domestic health objectives, even in the case of the apparently quite different assessments of multiple contributions. To the extent that the other reviewers did record a disproportionately large number of small contribution responses and consequently interpreted some, great, and maximal contribution somewhat differently than did the single reviewer, an adjustment for this phenomenon would bring the two assessments much closer than that implied in Table 4-4.

In order to assess the potential impact of the program in the several agencies on the U.S. domestic health objectives, the responses of the American reviewers were grouped by agency. These data are summarized for the single Harvard reviewer in Table 4-6 and for the other Harvard reviewers in Table 4-7.

The characteristics that were identified for the overall program responses seem to prevail at the agency level as well. The other reviewers display the same patterns of ranking projects more favorably and rating more projects as making multiple contributions. This holds for each of the agencies. There is an agency difference between the reviewers. The responses of the single reviewer display a marked tendency to rate HSMHA projects more favorably and NIH projects less favorably than the other reviewers, at all levels of contribution. The major difference among the agencies implied by the data in Tables 4-6 and 4-7 is that the responses of each reviewer tend to reflect relatively more HSMHA and FDA projects with multiple contributions. NIH projects are more often rated to contribute to fewer U.S. domestic health objectives. This would appear to be consistent with the types of research that are supported by the different agencies.

The essence of the relative potential impacts of the several agencies is summarized in Table 4-8. The relative shares of the agencies are outlined in the first two columns. First, the share of the agency is represented by its projects as a proportion of the 110 projects. Then the agency share is given as the proportion its total budget to date is of the total budget of the program. The data from the two previous tables are summarized in the last three columns to reflect the relative proportions of projects with different levels of contribution accounted for by the four agencies. These data provide certain important insights.

If the percent of projects with different potential impacts are compared with the percent of all projects the comparison is unfavorable to NIH, particularly in terms of projects with potential significant contributions. HSMHA and FDA, on the other hand, compare rather favorably. HSMHA is rated especially well in terms of projects with potential significant contributions.

Such comparisons, however, do not allow for the significant differences in the size of project budgets and the length of projects that were outlined in Chapter 3. It seems reasonable to expect more expensive projects, and perhaps longer-lived projects as well, to make correspondingly more contribution. Certainly the relevant assessment of impact is more appropriately the potential contribution per dollar expended. In these terms, the programs of NIH and FDA do somewhat better; the program of HSMHA less well. The relative position of HSMHA would be somewhat less unfavorable if an adjustment were made for the propensity of HSMHA projects to make multiple contributions but nonetheless, the apparent difference in relative potential impact is worthy of some consideration.

Table 4-6
Summary of the Number of Projects by the Number of U.S. Domestic Health Objectives for Which They Have Potential Contributions by Agency (Single Harvard Reviewer)

Number of Domestic Health Objectives Contributed to	Maximal or Great Contribution				Maximal, Great or Some Contribution				Any Contribution			
	NIH	HSMHA	FDA	EPA	NIH	HSMHA	FDA	EPA	NIH	HSMHA	FDA	EPA
0	31	61	7	1	18	28	2	—	11	9	1	—
1	1	7	—	—	9	24	2	1	10	24	1	1
2	—	1	—	—	3	10	1	—	5	20	2	—
3	—	—	—	—	—	3	1	—	1	8	2	—
4	—	1	—	—	2	2	1	—	4	4	1	—
5	—	—	—	—	—	2	—	—	—	1	—	—
6	—	—	—	—	—	1	—	—	1	4	—	—
7	—	—	—	—	—	—	—	—	—	—	—	—
8	—	—	—	—	—	—	—	—	—	—	—	—
9	—	—	—	—	—	—	—	—	—	—	—	—
10	—	—	—	—	—	—	—	—	—	—	—	—
Total number of projects	32	70	7	1	32	70	7	1	32	70	7	1

Table 4-7

Summary of the Number of Projects by the Number of U.S. Domestic Health Objectives for Which They Have Potential Contributions by Agency (Other Harvard Reviewers)

Number of Domestic Health Objectives Contributed to	Maximal or Great Contribution				Maximal, Great or Some Contribution				Any Contribution			
	NIH	HSMHA	FDA	EPA	NIH	HSMHA	FDA	EPA	NIH	HSMHA	FDA	EPA
0	23	39	3	—	11	21	—	—	4	5	—	—
1	2	9	1	1	11	5	1	—	6	7	—	—
2	1	13	1	—	2	5	—	—	2	2	1	—
3	5	5	—	—	2	13	1	—	2	16	—	—
4	—	—	1	—	4	8	3	—	10	5	1	—
5	1	4	—	—	2	8	1	1	4	9	1	1
6	—	—	1	—	—	9	—	—	4	8	2	—
7	—	—	—	—	—	—	1	—	—	9	2	—
8	—	—	—	—	—	—	—	—	—	6	—	—
9	—	—	—	—	—	—	—	—	—	1	—	—
10	—	—	—	—	—	1	—	—	—	2	—	1
Total number of projects	32	70	7	1	32	70	7	1	32	70	7	1

Table 4-8

A Comparison of Relative Agency Proportions of All Projects, Total Program Budget, and Number of Projects with Different Levels of Potential Contribution

Agency	Percent of		Percent of Projects with					
	All Projects	Program Budget to Date	Maximal or Great Contribution		Maximal, Great or Some Contribution		Any Contribution	
			S	H	S	H	S	H
NIH	29	19.3	10	20	23	27	24	28
HSMHA	64	75.4	90	69	68	63	68	64
FDA	6	5.1	–	9	8	9	7	7
EPA	1	0.2	–	2	1	1	1	1
Total	100	100.0	100	100	100	100	100	100

*Impact on Yugoslav Domestic Health
Objectives*

In order to assess the impact of the Special Foreign Currency Program on the Yugoslav domestic health objectives the Yugoslav reviewers were asked to rate the actual contribution for completed projects or the potential contribution for uncompleted projects to each of the ten health objectives. The questions that they responded to listed the same ten objectives as those that the American reviewers responded to. It would have been more appropriate to have a set of questions based on the Yugoslav domestic health objectives, but such a list had not been derived when the review process began. (Actually, there is much in common between the U.S. and Yugoslav domestic health objectives. This can be verified by a comparison of the U.S. domestic health objectives outlined in Table 2-2 [p. 15] and the Yugoslav domestic health objectives outlined in Table 3-13 [p. 41].) A summary of their responses is outlined in Table 4-9. The same qualifications that applied to the interpretation of the American responses in the previous section are relevant to the interpretation of the Yugoslav responses.

The Yugoslav team completed an evaluation of the impact of the Special Foreign Currency Program in Yugoslavia and submitted a separate report. (A brief overview of their report is presented on pp. 145-149.) It is of some interest to briefly compare the Yugoslav responses with the American responses concerning the contributions of the program to the domestic health objectives of their respective countries.

The first aspect of some interest involves the assessment of which health objectives are more likely and which less likely to be affected by the Special Foreign Currency Program in each country. In fact there is significant similiarity between the two countries in this regard according to the separate assessments.

Table 4-9

Summary of Yugoslav Reviewers' Assessment of the Actual or Potential Contribution to Yugoslav Domestic Health Objectives of the Special Foreign Currency Program in Yugoslavia

Objectives	Contribution									
	Maximal	Great	Some	Small	None	Not Known	Not Applicable	No Answer	Total	Mean (1)
Curing diseases	0	10	50	19	9	1	22	0	111	3.31
Morbidity reduction	0	13	42	24	3	2	27	0	111	3.21
Preventive health care advances	4	42	36	11	2	1	15	0	111	2.63
Promote positive health life	2	16	45	13	1	1	33	0	111	2.94
Improved geriatric care	0	5	24	14	13	2	53	0	111	3.63
Improved treatment of mental disorders	2	10	17	14	11	2	55	0	111	3.41
Efficient health services delivery	1	14	47	24	6	1	18	0	111	3.22
Equitable and efficient costing arrangements	0	9	36	25	12	2	27	0	111	3.49
Solutions to environmental problems	1	28	31	21	5	1	24	0	111	3.01
Improved health information	2	24	47	23	2	1	12	0	111	2.99
	12	171	375	188	64	14	286	0	1110	3.15

Of the five health objectives ranked highest in the two cases in terms of potential contributions from the program, four are common to both: Preventive Health Care Advances, Improved Health Information, Morbidity Reduction, and Solutions to the Problems associated with industrialization, urbanization, population growth, and environmental impairment. Further, the Yugoslav reviewers have ranked the same health objectives lowest in terms of potential impact that their American counterparts did. Both consider Improved Geriatric Care, Improved Treatment of Mental Disorders, and Equitable and Efficient Costing Arrangements to be the objectives that are least likely to be affected in the respective countries.

In terms of the proportion of projects that have potential for impact, the Yugoslav reviewers' responses reflect significantly more optimism for their country than did the Harvard reviewers for the United States. The Yugoslavs rate seventy projects to have potential for significant contributions to at least one health objective. Further, they rate 105 of the 110 with potential for some contribution to at least one health objective. Albeit the reviewers are answering different questions, it would appear that the Yugoslavs did in fact rate the projects much more favorably than the Harvard reviewers did.

Finally, the data in Table 4-10 provide a basis for comparing the assessments of the two teams in terms of multiple contributions. (The data in Table 4-10 for Yugoslav responses are comparable to the data in Table 4-4 for American responses.) Again there would appear to be a significant difference between the two teams. The Yugoslav reviewers clearly credit more projects with potential for multiple contributions.

It would be inappropriate to simply make the comparisons implicit in these data and draw the conclusion that the Special Foreign Currency Program has significantly more potential impact on Yugoslav domestic health objectives than on U.S. domestic health objectives. Such may be the case, but there are so many factors that may affect the absolute rankings that it is more appropriate to concentrate on the relative rankings. (Recall that the Yugoslav responses generally were more favorable to the questions outlined earlier in this chapter.) There is some reason, however, to infer that the relative impact in Yugoslavia may be somewhat higher. Both Yugoslav and American reviewers, it should be recalled, rated the relative importance of the diseases, disorders, or conditions studied by the program's projects to be somewhat more important for Yugoslavia than for the United States. Further, American and Yugoslav reviewers also considered the potential impact of the program to be somewhat higher for both the Yugoslav scientific establishment and health care system. Given those assessments, it is not unlikely that the potential impact of the program on the domestic health objectives is higher for Yugoslavia.

Additional Information

Time lags between most research activities and the actual impact of the research are to be expected. There is often some lag between the time that research is

Table 4-10

Summary of the Number of Projects by the Number of Yugoslav Domestic Health Objectives for Which They Have Potential Contribution

Number of Domestic Health Objectives Contributed to	Number of Projects with		
	Maximal or Great Contribution	Maximal, Great or Some Contribution	Any Contribution
0	40	5	4
1	24	6	2
2	16	5	4
3	15	13	0
4	1	20	10
5	6	16	10
6	6	12	16
7	1	15	19
8	1	8	19
9	–	4	12
10	–	6	14
	110	110	110

actually completed and the findings appear in the relevant literature. Further, there is usually some lag between the publication of research results and the general adoption of their implications. The Harvard reviewers were asked how long it would be before the results of a project would effect improvements in domestic health practice at a significant level if the results were published in an American scientific or professional journal. Their responses:

	S	H	Total
1. Immediately	1	8	9
2. After a short time	4	5	9
3. After a moderate time	15	36	51
4. After a long time	20	43	63
5. Never	22	9	31
6. Not known	5	3	8
7. Not applicable	41	7	48
No answer	2	1	3
	110	112	222
Mean (1)	3.94	3.40	3.60
Mean (2)	4.39	3.54	3.96

They were also asked how long it would be before the results would effect improvements in domestic health practice at a significant level if the results were published only in an official project report by HEW. Their responses:

	S	H	Total
1. Immediately	1	7	8
2. After a short time	3	12	15
3. After a moderate time	17	30	47
4. After a long time	20	19	39
5. Never	22	30	52
6. Not known	5	3	8
7. Not applicable	40	11	51
No answer	2	0	2
	110	112	222
Mean (1)	3.94	3.54	3.64
Mean (2)	4.38	3.72	4.00

The most striking thing about the responses of the reviewers concerning the time lag between publication and impact is the similarity in the potential of private and government publication. Apparently, the reviewers implicitly assume that HEW publication of research findings is a comparable alternative to publication in scientific and professional journals. If this is in fact the case, it may have rather significant policy implications for improving the potential impact of the program. (The Yugoslav reviewers were asked to answer essentially the same question within the context of Yugoslavia. Their answers reflected a clear advantage for publications in scientific and professional journals. This contrast is quite interesting.)

At the end of each questionnaire the reviewer was asked to indicate how much confidence he would place upon the answers he gave for the specific project reviewed. The responses were:

	S	H	Y	Total
1. Extreme confidence	2	4	3	9
2. Reasonable confidence	74	69	103	246
3. Moderate confidence	24	33	5	62
4. Some confidence	6	6	0	12
5. Little confidence	2	0	0	2
No answer	2	0	0	2
	110	112	111	333

These responses are about what might be expected. It is quite probable that the fact that a majority of projects were uncompleted introduced a degree of uncertainty that served to lower the level of reviewer confidence somewhat.

Given the nature of the three sets of responses, differences might have been expected. Since the other Harvard reviewers included nine individuals with varied backgrounds and expertise, for example, one might expect their confidence to be somewhat higher than that of the single Harvard reviewer. They were more likely than he was to be reviewing a project that fell within the boundaries of their specific expertise. The distinct similarity in the confidence levels of the single Harvard reviewer and the other Harvard reviewers implies that the uncertainty associated with incomplete projects may well serve to compensate for specific as opposed to general expertise.

The somewhat higher confidence of the Yugoslav reviewers may be associated with the general approach they employed in the review process, or it may reflect the advantage they had in having the opportunity to interview the project directors, or both.

On balance, the level of confidence in their responses as assessed subjectively by the reviewers is quite appropriate.

**Systematic Comparisons of the
Questionnaire Responses**

In all there were 56 responses for each of three reviewers for each of 110 projects. Thus, the questionnaires provided a large body of data that can be analyzed further to gain insights to such questions as: Are there systematic differences among the several agencies? Are there differences among the project types? Which types of projects are relatively better? What are the differential potential impacts of different types of projects? What factors in the operation of a project make it potentially of more relative value?

Some insights can be gained by comparing the reviewers' responses by agency and by type of project for relevant questions. The mean responses of all reviewers to specific representative relevant questions by agency and by project type are outlined in Tables 4-11 and 4-12, respectively.

A further analysis of this large body of data involved a correlation analysis of the responses and provides additional insights. The correlation analysis is straightforward and serves to uncover several important interactions among the variables that are relevant to the potential impact of the program.

Prior to the calculation of a correlation matrix, the responses of the several reviewers were standardized. This was done primarily to account for any systematic differences in subjective interpretation of the terms in which the responses were couched. Thus, systematic subjective differences among reviewers have been eliminated, but the comparative rankings by each reviewer across the projects reviewed have been preserved.

The formula for standardizing the responses of each reviewer was:

$$\text{Standardized Response} = \overline{X}_{sji} + C\frac{X_{jik} - \overline{X}_{ij}}{\text{S.D.}_{ij}}$$

Table 4-11

Mean Responses to Representative Relevant Questions for All Reviewers by Agency[a]

Response	HSMHA	NIH	FDA
Reasonable progress[b]	1.11	1.06	1.21
Cost overruns[b]	1.63	1.81	2.00
Proposed objectives relative to budget allocated	2.13	2.14	1.95
Actual accomplishments relative to budget allocated	2.42	2.18	2.42
Specific advantages of implementing in Yugoslavia	2.40	2.86	2.95
Relative importance for Yugoslavia of disease, disorder, or condition studied	2.61	2.95	2.59
Relative importance for U.S. of disease, disorder, or condition studied	2.92	2.90	2.48
Comparison of project with comparable research projects	2.71	2.68	3.00
U.S. nonfinancial contributions	2.97	3.18	3.29
Third-country contributions	4.23	4.50	4.91
Contribution to Yugoslav scientific establishment	3.47	2.83	3.09
Contribution to Yugoslav health care system	3.40	4.31	3.29
Contribution to U.S. scientific establishment	4.27	3.62	3.89
Contribution to U.S. health care system	4.03	4.65	3.50
Contribution to stimulation of further research	3.06	2.85	3.14
Contribution to knowledge	3.24	3.10	2.82
Unanticipated project benefits[b]	1.91	1.91	1.95
Reviewer's confidence	2.19	2.39	2.27

[a]The mean responses are those calculated as Mean (1) in the previous section; i.e., the not known and not applicable answers are ignored and the mean response calculated for the remaining responses.

[b]The answers were Yes or No, coded 1 or 2, respectively.

where $\overline{X}_{sji}$ is the mean response of the single reviewer to question j for those projects reviewed by reviewer i,

C is a constant,

X_{ijk} is the original response of reviewer i to question j for project k,

X_{ij} is the mean response of reviewer i to question j,

$S.D._{ij}$ is the standard deviation of reviewer i to question j.

Hence, the responses have been standardized by question and the resulting correlations represent an average correlation with each reviewer's correlation implicitly weighted to account for the proportion of projects reviewed but unaffected by the variance of the responses. (Correlation matrixes of the responses of all reviewers, Harvard reviewers, and Yugoslav reviewers are included in the Appendix [pp. 165-175].)

Certain other information, such as budget size and project length by project type and by agency, as were outlined in Chapter 3, are also available and in conjunction with the correlations uncovered contribute to a more systematic analysis of the program.

Specific Advantage of Yugoslavia

In the previous section it was noted that in terms of whether or not the specific projects could be implemented in Yugoslavia to some advantage over implementing them in the United States, the reviewers rated the program between some advantage and great advantage. Further analysis indicates certain differences among projects. First, more recent projects have less such advantage on average than projects that were started during the earlier years of the program. Perhaps the projects with some specific advantages were limited in number and type, or perhaps less attention is currently being given to the advantage of implementing a project in Yugoslavia in the approval process.

HSMHA projects tend to be rated as having more specific advantage in Yugoslavia. This is related to a similar rating for epidemiological research— HSMHA funds a disproportionate share of the epidemiological research. These findings are not surprising. Presumably, laboratory research would not in general be expected to have specific advantages when implemented in Yugoslavia. This is certainly consistent with the rating of laboratory research projects as having the least specific advantage in Yugoslavia. The relative ratings of the agencies undoubtedly reflect the relative proportions of the different project types supported by each agency.

Responses to a number of questions were significantly correlated[b] with responses to the advantages of implementing projects in Yugoslavia rather than in the United States. The relative importance for Yugoslavia of the disease, disorder, or condition studied was among these, as were the proposed objectives relative to budget allocated, potential impact on the U.S. health care system, and the reviewer's comparison of the project with comparable research projects known to him. In essence, if projects are supported that deal with diseases, disorders, or conditions that are priority ones in Yugoslavia the project can be implemented to more advantage in Yugoslavia. Further, these projects are more likely to attract the better Yugoslav researchers. These factors may explain the higher proposed benefits relative to the budget allocated and the higher potential these projects have for impact on the U.S. health care system.

[b]The correlations referred to as significant are those that are significant at the .001, .01, and .05 levels of confidence. Perhaps a note of caution concerning the significance of these correlation coefficients is in order at the outset. It is appropriate to use an especially strict level of significance whenever such a large number of correlations are calculated from a body of data. Further, the nature of the study and the data employed are such that the evaluation team prefers to interpret the statistics derived as conservatively as possible.

Table 4-12
Mean Responses to Representative Relevant Questions for All Reviewers by Project Type

Response	Laboratory Research	Laboratory and Epidemiological Research	Clinical Research	Clinical and Epidemiological Research	Epidemiological Research	Conference
Reasonable progress	1.09	1.06	1.14	1.03	1.19	1.00
Cost overruns	1.86	1.57	2.00	1.69	1.48	1.82
Proposed objectives relative to budget allocated	2.20	2.10	2.25	1.90	2.09	2.06
Actual accomplishments relative to budget allocated	2.15	2.20	2.67	2.36	2.58	2.13
Specific advantages of implementing in Yugoslavia	3.20	2.24	2.76	2.21	2.28	3.00
Relative importance for Yugoslavia of disease, disorder, or condition studied	3.21	3.10	2.90	2.41	2.44	2.50
Relative importance for U.S. of disease, disorder, or condition studied	3.32	3.50	3.00	2.61	2.69	2.68

Comparison of project with comparable research projects	3.17	2.25	2.75	2.62	2.64	3.00
U.S. nonfinancial contributions	3.20	3.14	3.60	2.82	2.89	2.30
Third-country contributions	4.71	4.11	5.00	4.26	4.33	2.76
Contribution to Yugoslav scientific establishment	2.70	3.19	3.52	3.28	3.34	3.61
Contribution to Yugoslav health care system	4.45	3.75	4.00	3.03	3.06	3.84
Contribution to U.S. scientific establishment	3.68	3.95	4.12	4.11	4.16	4.14
Contribution to U.S. health care system	4.77	4.31	4.38	3.66	4.03	4.33
Contribution to stimulation of further research	2.75	3.24	3.38	3.03	2.88	2.88
Contribution to knowledge	2.95	3.00	3.10	2.82	3.18	3.32
Unanticipated project benefits	1.89	1.95	1.95	2.00	1.85	1.88
Reviewer's confidence	2.46	2.19	2.48	2.13	2.20	2.18

Relative Progress of the Projects

It was noted in the previous section that the interpretation of what constitutes reasonable progress was clearly not the same among the several reviewers. In fact, there was a positive significant correlation between the responses to the specific questions concerning reasonable progress and the reviewer's confidence. Whatever the individual reviewer's criteria for reasonable progress, he has more confidence in his responses when they are met. (This should not be interpreted to mean that the individual reviewers are not individually consistent in terms of what constitutes reasonable progress. In fact, the negative correlation between cost overruns and reasonable progress, significant at the .01 level of confidence, implies a certain consistency.) Further, there was a negative significant correlation between reasonable progress and cost overruns.

In general, NIH projects were more often credited with having made reasonable progress in terms of the original time schedules than those of HSMHA. (Throughout this section the agency comparisons are made between NIH and HSMHA because their 32 and 70 projects respectively represent almost 93 percent of the data analyzed.) Again, the agency differences tend to be consonant with project type differences. As the mean responses in Table 4-12 imply, epidemiological projects generally were ranked lowest in terms of reasonable progress.

It was suggested that a comparison of proposed benefits with actual accomplishments might reflect the extent of reasonable progress. In fact, actual accomplishments were generally ranked somewhat lower than proposed objectives. (The only exception is worthy of note. Laboratory projects had a mean response of 2.15 for actual accomplishments and a mean response of 2.20 for proposed objectives.) To a certain extent this is to be expected. It is the nature of proposals to be optimistic. On the other hand, if certain characteristics are associated with higher-than-average actual accomplishments they ought to be promoted whenever possible.

Proposed objectives relative to budget allocated was significantly correlated with actual accomplishments in relation to budget, and emphasizes the obvious, that care should be exercised to select good projects to support. Of more significance, however, the only response that was significantly correlated with the reviewers' rating of actual accomplishments that represents a factor subject to policy manipulation was the extent of U.S. nonfinancial contributions. This would appear to be of signal importance. Nonfinancial contributions when made generally took the form of scientific guidance and methodological support. More benefits are more likely to be realized sooner when requisite assistance is provided. Project officers should be familiarized with the kinds of scientific guidance and methodological support that the Yugoslav project directors would benefit from most often, and attempt to have it provided.

The Relative Importance of the Projects

The reviewers rated the relative importance of the diseases, disorders, and conditions studied slightly more than important for the United States and somewhat more important for Yugoslavia. In fact, the correlation between the relative importance in the two countries was quite high and significant at the .001 level of confidence.

The relative importance for the United States of the diseases, disorders, or conditions studied was significantly correlated with a number of responses. All of these correlations are consistent with obvious relationships and require no specific explanation. The proposed objectives relative to budget allocated, the prevalance and incidence in the United States, and the potential contribution to several U.S. health objectives were all correlated significantly with the response of relative importance for the United States.

The same general pattern of correlations occurred for the relative importance for Yugoslavia of the diseases, disorders, or conditions studied. The proposed objectives relative to budget allocated, the prevalence and incidence in Yugoslavia, and the potential contribution to several Yugoslav health objectives were all significantly correlated with the response of relative importance for Yugoslavia.

These correlations would be expected. The assessment of the program in terms of relative importance lies not in the correlations but rather in the ratings of the relative importance outlined in the previous section. (To satisfy oneself of this, one need only recognize that these significant correlations could come from a program with any proportion of projects that dealt with important problems. The correlations simply reflect high ratings in the several instances for projects that deal with relatively important problems and low ratings for projects that deal with relatively unimportant problems, and are invariant to whether there are more or less projects in either category.) The projects do tend to deal with important problems.

Comparable Research Projects

There was a significant correlation between the comparison of a project with comparable research projects and the specific advantages of implementing the project in Yugoslavia. This tends to reenforce the inferences already drawn that the program does relatively better in contexts where it concentrates on projects that can be implemented in Yugoslavia to some advantage.

In the same context, the reviewers' responses to how these projects compared with comparable research projects was significantly correlated with their ratings of the potential contribution to knowledge (at the .01 level of significance). This could simply mean that better projects will contribute more to scientific knowledge. On the other hand, it may be an indication that if the project has some specific advantage if implemented in Yugoslavia it will provide particularly unique research, or attract the better Yugoslav researchers who are more likely to make a contribution to knowledge, or both.

Cooperative Efforts

HSMHA projects tend to receive more nonfinancial contributions from the United States, and also receive contributions more often from parties other than the United States and Yugoslavia. Projects that involve epidemiological research tend to receive more U.S. nonfinancial contributions than other types of projects. The contributions are generally in the form of scientific guidance and methodological support. Assistance with data processing techniques is an example in point. As noted before, of course, these two are probably related. HSMHA funds proportionately more epidemiological research in Yugoslavia than other agencies. Of course, nonfinancial contributions are made by agencies other than HSMHA, and to project types other than epidemiological research.

These nonfinancial contributions probably have an effect on the program along certain dimensions. Nonfinancial contributions are significantly correlated with actual project accomplishments. Further, nonfinancial contributions are significantly correlated with the contribution to the development of Yugoslav health manpower, to both the U.S. and Yugoslav scientific establishments, to the stimulation of further research, and to several health objectives. Presumably, when scientific guidance or methodological support is given to a specific project it has somewhat broader, more general implications.

Finally, it should be noted that more recent projects have received less in the way of nonfinancial contributions. No particular conclusion is offered on the basis of this apparent phenomenon. It would be encouraging if earlier contributions of the program in general were currently reflected in less need for nonfinancial contributions by recently funded projects. It could, however, simply mean that the projects have had less time for such support to occur.

Nonfinancial contributions also have a financial implication, however. Nonfinancial contributions are significantly correlated with cost overruns (at the .01 level of significance). In fact, a number of factors are undoubtedly interacting in this context. HSMHA projects and especially epidemiological projects benefit more from nonfinancial contributions in general, but they also tend to be subject to more cost overruns. It is quite probable that projects that gain exposure through the process of nonfinancial contributions are more likely to receive favorable responses to requests for budgetary increases, particularly when such increases are based on the implications of suggestions by American project officers or consultants.

Albeit there is no basis for drawing a definitive conclusion at this point, it is important to note that the implication of the analysis is that considerable attention should be paid to the apparent phenomena in this context. It is certainly reasonable to hypothesize, for example, that nonfinancial contributions rendered at an early stage of a project might result in increased benefits at lower costs.

Project Impact

The general impact of the program has been gauged from the responses concerning the potential contributions to knowledge and the stimulation of further research, and the potential contributions to the Yugoslav scientific establishment, the Yugoslav health care system, the U.S. scientific establishment, and the U.S. health care system. The contributions to knowledge and the stimulation of further research were considered to be more than small by all reviewers and more than some by Yugoslav reviewers. In general, the impact on the scientific establishment was considered to be somewhat greater than the impact on the health care system for each country. Finally, the impact was generally considered to be somewhat less in the United States than it was in Yugoslavia.

The mean responses outlined in Tables 4-11 and 4-12 display consistent agency and project type differences in terms of general impact. On the one hand, NIH projects and laboratory projects are generally rated to have more potential for contributions to knowledge, to stimulation of further research, and to the scientific establishments of both countries. On the other hand, HSMHA projects and epidemiological projects are generally rated higher in terms of the potential for contribution to the health care systems of the two countries.

The correlation analysis provides some indication of the factors that are associated with the general impact of the projects.

The potential contribution to knowledge and the stimulation of further research are significantly correlated. In turn, both are significantly correlated with proposed objectives relative to budget allocated, the potential contribution to the scientific establishment of Yugoslavia, several health objectives in the two countries, and the potential impact on countries other than Yugoslavia or the United States. The potential contribution to knowledge is also significantly correlated with favorable comparisons to comparable research projects, while the potential stimulation of further research is significantly correlated with the potential contribution to the scientific establishment of the United States, actual accomplishments, and U.S. nonfinancial contributions.

On balance, the pattern of general impact that emerges from a consideration of contributions to knowledge and the stimulation of further research is that projects that deal with important diseases, disorders, and conditions, particularly projects that may provide new insights into coping with them, are viewed by the reviewers to have greater potential for impact on knowledge, further research, and the scientific establishment and, eventually, for making a contribution toward affecting those diseases, disorders, and conditions.

The correlation analysis also provides some indication of the general nature of the relative contributions to the scientific establishments and the health care systems of both countries. As noted above, laboratory research contributes more to the scientific establishment, while epidemiological research contributes more to the health care system. Similarly, NIH projects generally have more impact on the scientific establishment and HSMHA projects tend to have more impact on the health care system.

The same projects have the same potential impacts for both countries. Thus, for example, the contribution to the Yugoslav scientific establishment is very significantly correlated with the contribution to the U.S. scientific establishment. Similarly, the contributions to Yugoslav and U.S. health care systems are very significantly correlated. Further, the responses of the reviewers tend to imply specific tradeoffs between contributions to the scientific establishment and the health care system. There is a consistent pattern of negative correlations between the reviewers' responses of contributions to the scientific establishments and the health care systems. (Albeit none is statistically significant, there are negative correlations between contributions to U.S. scientific establishment and U.S. health care system, between contributions to Yugoslav scientific establishment and Yugoslav health care system, between U.S. scientific establishment and Yugoslav health care system, and between Yugoslav scientific establishment and U.S. health care system.) Finally, contributions to the scientific establishment and to the health care system tend to be correlated positively or negatively with specific health objectives in a rather systematic pattern.

Before the correlations specific to the impact on domestic health objectives are outlined it may be appropriate to digress briefly and reiterate the proper interpretation of the correlation analysis in general. It should be emphasized that the correlations are in fact among responses. The responses to the several questions are couched in the semi-quantitative terms maximal, great, some, small, and none. These responses are recorded as 1, 2, 3, 4, and 5, respectively. As outlined above, the correlations were calculated from the set of standardized responses.

A positive correlation will obtain whenever reviewers tend to respond with similar ratings for two questions. Thus, for example, the positive correlation between contributions to knowledge and the stimulation of further research obtains because whenever reviewers rate the contribution to knowledge for a project to be maximal or great they tend to rate the contributions to the stimulation of further research to be maximal or great, while whenever they rate small or no contribution for one they also tend to rate small or no contribution for the other.

A negative correlation, on the other hand, will reflect the tendency of reviewers to rate different questions at opposite ends of the scale. Thus, for example, the negative correlation between the contribution to the scientific establishment and the contribution to the health care system implies that those projects that were rated to have high contributions to the scientific establishment were rated to have low contributions to the health care system, while those that were rated to have high contributions to the health care system were rated to have low contributions to the scientific establishment.

The positive correlations simply reflect that high responses on one question are usually associated with high responses on the other, and vice versa. The negative correlations simply reflect that high responses on one question are associated with low responses on the other question, and vice versa. This is how the correlations should be interpreted. Some readers have an unfortunate tendency to interpret positive correlations as reflecting something good and negative correlations as reflecting something bad; but a negative correlation means that projects that contribute to the scientific establishment tend not to contribute to the health care system, not that they have a negative impact on it.

Impact on U.S. Domestic Health Objectives

The two evaluation teams were asked to consider the impact of the Special Foreign Currency Program in Yugoslavia on the domestic health objectives of their respective countries. Hence, for each project the Harvard reviewers and the Yugoslav reviewers were answering different questions when it came to rating the potential contribution to each of the ten health objectives. In order to gain the appropriate perspective, therefore, separate correlation analyses were done for the Harvard reviewers and the Yugoslav reviewers. The separate correlation matrices are included in the Appendix (pp. 168-175). The data analyzed in this section are the correlations among the responses of the Harvard reviewers.

The answers to two questions would seem to provide some insight to the issue of the impact of the program on the U.S. domestic health objectives. First, are there any systematic relationships among the ten objectives that can be inferred from the correlations among the reviewers' responses? Second, what are the factors which seem to be associated with each of the objectives or with related objectives?

The correlations among the reviewers' responses do seem to indicate certain systematic relationships among the U.S. domestic health objectives, at least in terms of the extent to which these reviewers tend to rate the contributions of the projects to the several objectives. These relationships are outlined in Table 4-13.

The relationship that is implied by the correlations among curing diseases, morbidity reduction, and improved geriatric care is a reasonable one. Clearly morbidity reduction is generally associated with curing diseases and the correla-

Table 4-13

Summary of Correlation Analysis of Harvard Reviewers' Responses: Correlations Among the U.S. Domestic Health Objectives

Objective	Correlated with Objectives*	Correlation Coefficient
Curing diseases	Morbidity reduction	.48
	Improved geriatric care	.36
Morbidity reduction	Curing diseases	.48
	Preventive health care advances	.60
	Improved geriatric care	.36
Preventive health care advances	Morbidity reduction	.60
	Promote positive health life	.43
	Solutions to environmental problems	.28
	Improved geriatric care	.37
Promote positive health life	Preventive health care advances	.43
	Solutions to environmental problems	.44
Improved geriatric care	Curing diseases	.36
	Morbidity reduction	.36
	Preventive health care advances	.37
Improved treatment of mental disorders	None	
Efficient health services delivery	None	
Equitable and efficient costing arrangements	None	
Solutions to environmental problems	Preventive health care advances	.40
	Promote positive health life	.44
Improved health information	None	

*Correlations significant at the .01 level.

tions imply that the potential contribution of the program to improved geriatric care is from curing diseases and affecting morbidity among the aged. The responses included many more projects making a contribution to curing diseases and morbidity reduction than to improved geriatric care, but the significant correlation indicates that those that are rated with a significant contribution to the latter also are rated with a significant contribution to both the former health objectives.

Morbidity reduction and improved geriatric care are also significantly correlated with preventive health care advances. It would appear that the reviewers' responses concerning a number of projects reflect the traditional expected relationship between preventive health care measures and reduced morbidity. Further, preventive health care advances are apparently viewed by the reviewers as having potential for benefiting the aged specifically.

The relationship implied by the correlations among preventive health care advances, solutions to environmental problems, and promotion of positive health life is also a reasonable one. Presumably many projects that contribute to preventive health care advances and solutions to environmental problems involve consumer education, nutritional improvements, and the like. Further, preventive health care measures and those which promote the positive health life, such as consumer education and nutritional improvements, apparently represent reasonable ways to cope with certain of the problems associated with trends in industrialization, urbanization, population growth, and environmental impairment.

There are no other systematic relationships among the U.S. domestic health objectives implicit in the correlations among the reviewers' responses. Contributions to improved treatment of mental disorders, efficient health services delivery, equitable and efficient costing arrangements, and improved health information are not correlated with contributions to other objectives.

It might be noted that there is actually a subtle relationship between the two objectives of efficient health services delivery and equitable and efficient costing arrangements. Efficient costing arrangements are likely to contribute to efficient health services delivery in the sense of the term implicit in economic efficiency and perhaps in the sense of the term implicit in technical efficiency. Equitable costing arrangements are quite a different matter. Most costing arrangements that would generally be considered equitable would have an adverse effect on economic efficiency, and perhaps on technical efficiency as well. It is unlikely that many of the reviewers had this subtle relationship in mind. Fortunately, there are so few projects that were considered to have much to do with equitable and efficient costing arrangements that no particular problem was introduced for the analysis. In fact the single Harvard reviewer had no projects ranked as making any contribution to equitable and efficient costing arrangements. The other Harvard reviewers ranked five making a small contribution, five making some contribution, and one making a great contribution.

Improved health information is distinct. There is no significant correlation between this objective and any other among the responses of the reviewers. Presumably, a variety of projects that make contributions to various of the other objectives provide health information, but there is apparently no systematic relationship between the relative contribution of a project to any of the other objectives and the relative importance of the contribution to the pool of health information, in the assessment of the reviewers.

Identifying the systematic relationship among the ten objectives implicit in the reviewers' responses is important in the sense that some insight is gained to the pattern of their responses. Clearly a better perspective is now available on the issue of multiple contributions, for example. Apparently the multiple contributions tend to cluster in groups. Multiple contributions at approximately the same level of contribution tend to be recorded among curing diseases, morbidity reduction, and improved geriatric care, and among preventive health care advances, solutions to environmental problems, and promotion of positive health life. If multiple contributions are recorded for projects that deal with the other objectives they tend to be for quite different levels of contribution. Understanding the patterns that prevail enhances any interpretation of the reviewers' responses.

The second, and perhaps more important, question concerns the factors that can be inferred from the correlation analysis to be associated with each of the objectives or with related objectives. The significant correlations between the several U.S. domestic health objectives and other responses of the Harvard reviewers are summarized in Table 4-14. These data in fact imply that three factors tend to dominate the ratings of the contributions to U.S. domestic health objectives by the reviewers—the relative importance of the problem studied, the potential impact the results will have on the health care system, and the potential contribution the project will make to the scientific establishment. Further, there are differences among the objectives in terms of whether they are associated with one or more of the factors.

First, there are a number of responses that indicate relative importance directly. The relative importance for Yugoslavia and the relative importance for the United States of the disease, disorder, or condition studied clearly reflect the relative importance of the problem. Similarly the U.S. prevalence and the U.S. incidence reflect relative importance directly. Second, there are responses that reflect the apparent assessment of the reviewers of the potential impact the results will have on the health care system—the impact on the U.S. health care

Table 4-14

Summary of Correlation Analysis of Harvard Reviewers' Responses: Correlations Between U.S. Domestic Health Objectives and Other Responses

Objective	Correlated Most Significantly with Responses	Correlation Coefficient	Level of Significance
Curing diseases	Contribution to knowledge	.49	.001
	Stimulation of further research	.29	.01
	Impact on Yugoslav scientific establishment	.27	.01
Morbidity reduction	Contribution to knowledge	.41	.001
	Proposed benefits	.37	.001
	Impact on other countries	.36	.001
	Stimulation of further research	.29	.01
	Impact on U.S. scientific establishment	.27	.01
Preventive health care advances	Proposed benefits	.44	.001
	Impact on other countries	.38	.001
	Impact on U.S. health care system	.35	.001
	Relative importance for Yugoslavia	.35	.001

Table 4-14 (cont.)

Objective	Correlated Most Significantly with Responses	Correlation Coefficient	Level of Significance
	Relative importance for U.S.	.34	.001
	Impact on Yugoslav health care system	.32	.001
Promote positive health life	Relative importance for Yugoslavia	.32	.01
	Impact on Yugoslav health care system	.30	.01
	Relative importance for U.S.	.29	.01
	Impact on other countries	.27	.01
Improved geriatric care	U.S. nonfinancial contributions	.37	.001
	Impact on other countries	.36	.001
	Stimulation of further research	.35	.001
	Impact on U.S. scientific establishment	.35	.001
	Contribution to knowledge	.32	.001
Improved treatment of mental disorders	Unanticipated project benefits	.34	.001
	Impact on Yugoslav scientific establishment	.31	.001
	Impact on U.S. scientific establishment	.28	.01
Efficient health services delivery	Impact on Yugoslav health care system	.66	.001
	Impact on U.S. health care system	.54	.001
	Impact on U.S. scientific establishment	−.25	.01
	Impact on Yugoslav scientific establishment	−.20	.05
Equitable and efficient costing arrangements	Impact on other countries	.26	.01
	Impact on U.S. manpower	−.30	.01
	Actual accomplishments	−.26	.05
	Impact on U.S. scientific establishment	−.22	.05
Solutions to environmental problems	Impact on other countries	.29	.01
	Relative importance for Yugoslavia	.21	.05
	Impact on Yugoslav health care system	.21	.05
Improved health information	Impact on U.S. scientific establishment	.35	.001
	Impact on Yugoslav scientific establishment	.33	.001
	Stimulation of further research	.32	.001
	U.S. incidence	.28	.05
	U.S. prevalence	.26	.05

system and the impact on the Yugoslav health care system. Third, there are responses that represent the assessment of the reviewers of the potential contribution the projects will make to the scientific establishment—the impact on the U.S. scientific establishment and the impact on the Yugoslav scientific establishment. Finally, there are certain responses which might reflect any of the three and can only be interpreted in context. The proposed benefits, the contribution to knowledge, the stimulation of further research, and the impact on other countries might derive from the relative importance of the problem studied, the potential impact on the health care system of the results, the contribution to the scientific establishment, any two, or all three. The general pattern that is implied by the correlations between the ten objectives and other responses is summarized in Table 4-15.

The factors correlated significantly with the objectives of curing diseases and morbidity reduction display a rather singular pattern. Virtually all the responses significantly correlated with these two objectives can be interpreted as indications of the reviewers' assessments of the potential contribution the project will make to the scientific establishment. No response that would indicate relative importance or that would imply impact on the health care system is correlated

Table 4-15
Implied Associations Among U.S. Domestic Health Objectives and the Relative Importance of Problem Studied, the Potential Impact of Results on the Health Care System, and the Potential Impact on the Scientific Establishment

	Associated with		
Objective	Relative Importance	Impact on Health Care System	Impact on Scientific Establishment
Curing diseases	No	No	Yes
Morbidity reduction	No	No	Yes
Preventive Health care advances	Yes	Yes	No
Promote positive health life	Yes	Yes	No
Improved geriatric care	Yes	Yes	Yes
Improved treatment of mental disorders	No	No	Yes
Efficient health services delivery	No	Yes	No
Equitable and efficient costing arrangements	No	No	No
Solutions to environmental problems	Yes	Yes	No
Improved health information	Yes	No	Yes

significantly with either objective. (In fact, there are negative correlations between curing disease and responses that indicate relative importance, such as relative importance in Yugoslavia, relative importance in the U.S., and U.S. incidence.) The implied relationship, or rather the absence of one, between the objectives of curing disease and reducing morbidity and the potential impact on the health care system is straightforward and consonant with expectations. In essence, the reviewers do not expect particular disease control to have a significant or general impact on the health care system. The lack of relationship between these objectives and relative importance suggests that the reviewers assess the potential contribution of the program to controlling disease to be more likely in the context of those diseases which are not among the most important in terms of such indications as incidence, prevalence, premature death, and excess morbidity.

The responses correlated with the objective of improved treatment of mental disorders display a similar pattern. All the responses significantly correlated with this objective indicate the reviewers' assessments of the potential impact on the scientific establishment. Further, the objective is negatively correlated with the impact on both health care systems and with the relative importance for Yugoslavia.

The factors correlated significantly with the objective of efficient health services delivery also display a singular pattern, but involve the potential impact of the results on the health care system. In fact, there is a significant negative correlation between this objective and the potential impact on the scientific establishments of both the United States and Yugoslavia, and no correlation between the objective and any response indicating relative importance. (The reader is reminded that the negative correlations obtain because projects that have a potential for contributions to efficient health services delivery have little or no potential for contributions to the scientific establishment, while those with potential for contributions to the scientific establishment have little or no impact on health services delivery; not because one has a negative impact on the other.)

The factors correlated with the objectives of preventive health care advances, promotion of positive health life, and solutions to environmental problems, on the other hand, display a dual pattern. Both the relative importance of the problem studied and the potential impact of the results on the health care system are associated with the reviewers' assessments of the potential contributions to these three objectives.

The objective equitable and efficient costing arrangements displays no relationship with any of the factors. There is a significant negative correlation between this objective and the reviewers' responses concerning impact on the U.S. scientific establishment. (There is also a negative but not significant correlation between the objective and the impact on the Yugoslav scientific establishment.) The correlations between equitable and efficient costing arrangements and all the responses that indicate relative importance are also negative, albeit insignificant. It would not be unreasonable to expect a relationship between the objective of equitable and efficient costing arrangements and the potential impact on the health care system, but in fact the correlations from which such a relationship would have to be inferred are quite low. Too few projects were ranked as making any contribution to this objective to warrant drawing any specific conclusions.

The objective of improved geriatric care would appear to be related to all three factors—relative importance, impact on the health care system, and impact on the scientific establishment. In addition to the correlations outlined in Table 4-14, the objective of improved geriatric care was also significantly correlated with other responses including the relative importance in the United States, U.S. prevalence, and the potential impact on the U.S. health care system (all at the .05 level of significance). This singular pattern is consistent with the systematic relationships among the health objectives that were outlined above. Improved geriatric care was correlated with the related objectives of curing diseases and reducing morbidity on the one hand, and the objective of preventive health care advances on the other. It seems likely that the association between improved geriatric care and the impact on the scientific establishment derives from its relationship with curing disease and morbidity reduction, while its association with relative importance and impact on the health care system derives from its relationship with preventive health care advances.

Finally, improved health information remains distinct. Potential contributions to improved health information are associated with relative importance and potential impact on the scientific establishment, but not with potential impact on the health care system. That the reviewers tend to rate health information for its cumulative value to health research is indicated by the very significant correlations between improved health information and the potential impact on the U.S. scientific establishment, the potential impact on the Yugoslav scientific establishment, and the stimulation of further research. The association between the objective of improved health information and relative importance emphasizes the obvious—the relative importance of information increases with the relative importance of the problem.

The correlation analysis has in fact provided a significant perspective of the assessment by the Harvard reviewers of the impact of the program on the U.S. domestic health objectives. Certain relationships among the ten objectives can be inferred from the correlations among them. Curing diseases and morbidity reduction are related objectives in the assessments of the reviewers, as are the objectives of preventive health care advances, promotion of positive health life, and solutions to environmental problems. The objective of improved geriatric care is correlated with the related objectives of curing diseases and morbidity on the one hand, and with the objective of preventive health care advances on the other hand. None of the remaining four objectives—improved treatment of mental disorders, efficient health services delivery, equitable and efficient costing arrangements, and improved health information—are systematically related to any other health objective.

Further, the correlation analysis implies that three factors tend to dominate the reviewers' ratings of the contributions to U.S. domestic health objectives, and that certain differences exist among the objectives in terms of this association with these factors. First, the potential contribution to the scientific establishment tends to dominate the rankings of three health objectives—curing diseases, morbidity reduction, and improved treatment of mental disorders. Second, the reviewers' assessment of the potential impact on the health care system would appear to dominate their rankings of the objective of efficient health services delivery. Third, both the relative importance of the problem and the potential impact on the health care system are associated with the rankings of the related health objectives of preventive health care advances, promotion of positive health life, and solutions to environmental problems. Fourth, two factors are also associated with the rankings of the objective improved health information. In this case, however, the two factors are the relative importance of the problem and the potential impact on the scientific establishment. Fifth, all three factors are associated with the rankings of the objective improved geriatric care. Finally, none of the factors are associated with the rankings of the objective of equitable and efficient costing arrangements.

On balance, the patterns of related objectives and associations tend to reenforce one another and lend credence to the inference of each.

Impact on Yugoslav Domestic Health Objectives

Since separate correlation analyses were done for the Harvard and Yugoslav reviewers, it is possible to make certain comparisons between the relationships and associations inferred from the correlations among the responses of each. These comparisons can provide additional insight into the assessments of the contribution of the Special Foreign Currency Program to the domestic health objectives of the two countries.

In order to facilitate these comparisons, the correlation analysis of the Yugoslav responses is summarized in Tables 4-16, 4-17, and 4-18. The data in these tables correspond to the data summarized for the Harvard responses in the previous section. How do they compare?

First, comparing the Yugoslav data in Table 4-16 with the Harvard data in Table 4-13, there appear to be no systematic differences in the size of the correlation coefficients among the several health objectives. A difference that can be inferred is that the Yugoslav responses reflect generally more related objectives. The Harvard responses implied four objectives that were not, directly at least, related to any other objective. The Yugoslav responses imply that each

Table 4-16

Summary of Correlation Analysis of Yugoslav Responses: Correlations Among Yugoslav Domestic Health Objectives

Objective	Correlated with Objectives*	Correlation Coefficient
Curing diseases	Preventive health care advances	.31
	Promote positive health life	.33
	Improved geriatric care	.45
Morbidity reduction	Preventive health care advances	.58
Preventive health care advances	Curing diseases	.31
	Morbidity reduction	.58
	Promote positive health life	.40
	Solutions to environmental problems	.46
Promote positive health life	Curing diseases	.33
	Preventive health care advances	.40
	Solutions to environmental problems	.42
Improved geriatric care	Curing diseases	.45
	Improved treatment of mental disorders	.54
Improved treatment of mental disorders	Improved geriatric care	.54
Efficient health services delivery	Equitable and efficient costing arrangements	.50
	Improved health information	.28
Equitable and efficient costing arrangements	Efficient health services delivery	.50
	Solutions to environmental problems	.33
	Improved health services delivery	.50
Solutions to environmental problems	Preventive health care advances	.46
	Promote positive health life	.42
	Equitable and efficient costing arrangements	.33
Improved health information	Efficient health services delivery	.28
	Equitable and efficient costing arrangements	.45

*Correlations significant at the .01 level.

objective is related to at least one other objective. In most cases, the Yugoslav responses imply the relationships implied by the Harvard responses, plus additional relationships. The only exceptions to this general tendency are that curing diseases and morbidity reduction are not correlated, and improved geriatric care is not related to morbidity reduction and preventive health care advances.

This phenomenon of more relationships among the several objectives implicit in the correlation analysis of the Yugoslav responses does provide an insight into

Table 4-17

Summary of Correlation Analysis of Yugoslav Responses: Correlations Between Yugoslav Domestic Health Objectives and Other Responses

Objective	Correlated Most Significantly with Responses	Correlation Coefficient	Level of Significance
Curing diseases	Impact on Yugoslav scientific establishment	.31	.01
	Impact on Yugoslav health manpower	.30	.01
Morbidity reduction	Comparison with comparable research	.42	.05
	Impact on Yugoslav health care system	.27	.05
Preventive health care advances	Impact on Yugoslav health care system	.35	.001
	Impact on U.S. health care system	.42	.01
	Specific advantage in Yugoslavia	.32	.01
	Relative importance for U.S.	.27	.05
	Impact on Yugoslav scientific establishment	−.26	.05
	Impact on Yugoslav health manpower	.24	.05
Promote positive health life	Impact on U.S. health care system	.37	.05
Improved geriatric care	Impact on U.S. scientific establishment	.53	.001
	Impact on Yugoslav scientific establishment	.39	.01
	Stimulation of further research	.30	.05
	Relative importance for U.S.	.29	.05
Improved treatment of mental disorders	Specific advantage in Yugoslavia	−.38	.01
	Impact on other countries	−.30	.01
Efficient health services delivery	Impact on Yugoslav health care system	.51	.001
	Impact on Yugoslav health manpower	.46	.001
	Third-country contributions	.38	.001
	Yugoslav prevalence	.33	.01
	Yugoslav incidence	.29	.05
	Impact on U.S. health care system	.30	.05
Equitable and efficient costing arrangements	Impact on Yugoslav health care system	.36	.01
	Impact on Yugoslav health manpower	.32	.01
	Specific advantage in Yugoslavia	.30	.01
	Relative importance to Yugoslavia	.24	.05

Table 4-17 (cont.)

Objective	Correlated Most Significantly with Responses	Correlation Coefficient	Level of Significance
Solutions to environmental problems	Relative importance to U.S.	.31	.01
	Specific advantage in Yugoslavia	.29	.01
	Relative importance to Yugoslavia	.27	.05
	Impact on Yugoslav scientific establishment	−.27	.05
Improved health information	Impact on U.S. health care system	.53	.001
	Impact on Yugoslav health care system	.30	.01
	Impact on other countries	.30	.01
	Impact on Yugoslav health manpower	.29	.01
	Stimulation of further research	.27	.01
	Impact on U.S. scientific establishment	.28	.05

Table 4-18
Implied Associations Among Yugoslav Domestic Health Objectives and the Relative Importance of Problem Studied, the Potential Impact of Results on the Health Care System, the Potential Impact on the Scientific Establishment, and the Impact on Health Manpower Development

	Associated with			
Objective	Relative Importance	Impact on Health Care System	Impact on Scientific Establishment	Impact on Health Manpower Development
Curing diseases	No	No	Yes	Yes
Morbidity reduction	No	Yes	No	No
Preventive health care advances	Yes	Yes	No	Yes
Promote positive health life	No	Yes	No	No
Improved geriatric care	Yes	No	Yes	No
Improved treatment of mental disorders	No	No	No	No
Efficient health services delivery	Yes	Yes	No	Yes
Equitable and efficient costing arrangements	Yes	Yes	No	Yes
Solutions to environmental problems	Yes	Yes	No	No
Improved health information	No	Yes	Yes	Yes

the difference between the assessments of the two teams of the contribution of the program to the domestic health objectives of each country. A significant difference was found between the two teams' assessments in terms of multiple contributions of projects to several objectives. The Yugoslav reviewers clearly credited more projects with potential for multiple contributions (see p. 68). The differences observed in terms of multiple contributions obviously derive in large part from the differences in relationships among objectives.

A comparison of the Yugoslav data in Tables 4-17 and 4-18 with the Harvard data in Tables 4-14 and 4-15 provides additional insights to other aspects of the assessments of the two teams outlined above. Both Yugoslav and Harvard reviewers rated the diseases, disorders, or conditions studied as somewhat more important for Yugoslavia than for the United States, for example (see p. 48). Further, in terms of the proportion of projects that have potential for impact, the Yugoslav reviewers' responses reflect significantly more optimism for their country than the Harvard reviewers' responses reflect for the United States (see p. 68).

The data in Table 4-17 imply that the same three factors that tended to dominate the ratings of the U.S. domestic health objectives by the Harvard reviewers are significantly associated with the ratings of the Yugoslav domestic health objectives by the Yugoslav reviewers. In addition, the contribution to Yugoslav health manpower development appears to be a significant factor associated with the ratings of the health objectives by the Yugoslav reviewers.

The data in Table 4-18 imply that certain differences obtain in terms of the factors that are associated with the several objectives in the ratings of the Yugoslav reviewers as compared with the associations inferred from the ratings of the Harvard reviewers. In fact, the factors correlated significantly with the objectives display the same pattern for only three of the ten objectives—the curing of diseases, preventive health care advances, and solutions to environmental problems.

There is a certain pattern to the differences implicit in a comparison of the associations between the factors and the remaining seven health objectives. For example, the impact on the scientific establishment is associated with fewer objectives by the Yugoslav reviewers than by the Harvard reviewers. On the other hand, however, the impact on the health care system is associated with more objectives by the Yugoslav reviewers than by the Harvard reviewers.

In the case of the impact on the scientific establishment, the difference is simply that the Yugoslav responses display an association with fewer objectives. Specifically, the impact on the scientific establishment is not associated with morbidity reduction and improved treatment of mental disorders, as it was for the responses of the Harvard reviewers. In the case of the impact on the health care system, the Yugoslav responses display an association with three objectives that the Harvard responses did not—morbidity reduction, equitable and efficient costing arrangements, and improved health information—and do not display an association with one objective that the Harvard responses did—improved geriatric care. On balance, it would appear that the Yugoslav reviewers associate contributions to the scientific establishment with fewer health objectives and potential impact on the health care system with more health objectives than do their Harvard counterparts.

There are also differences in the associations between the relative importance of the problem studied and certain of the health objectives. On the one hand, the Yugoslav ratings of the potential impacts on the objectives of efficient health services delivery and equitable and efficient costing arrangements are associated with relative importance, while the Harvard ratings on these objectives were not. On the other hand, the Yugoslav ratings of the potential impacts on the objectives of promoting a positive health life and improved health information are not associated with relative importance, while the Harvard ratings on these objectives were.

Some inferences may be drawn from these comparisons, but care should certainly be exercised in so doing, recalling what the correlations reflect. Thus, for example, more Yugoslav than U.S. health objectives are associated with responses that imply potential for impact on the health care system. In part, this apparent difference may reflect that the program has more potential for impact on the Yugoslav health care system than on that of the United States, but there is the distinct possibility that a major part of the difference is due to a difference in interpretation. The question of impact on the health care system was intended to be interpreted with the emphasis on the word system. As noted above (pp. 51-52), however, the actual distributions of responses to the question imply that all reviewers did not interpret this question the same way. Hence, the somewhat higher potential for impact on the health care system inferred from the Yugoslav correlations should to some extent be qualified.

Additional Information

The Harvard reviewers were asked how long it would be before the results of a project would effect improvements in domestic health practice at a significant level if published in an American scientific or professional journal or only in an official project report by HEW. The Yugoslav reviewers were asked to answer essentially the same question. The Harvard responses indicate an implicit assumption by the reviewers that HEW publication of research findings is a comparable alternative to publication in scientific and professional journals, but the Yugoslav responses reflect a clear advantage for publications in scientific and professional journals.

The correlations between the time lag from publication of results to impact and the other responses generally indicate a rather straightforward and pre-dictable pattern which requires little in the way of elaboration. The relative importance of the findings has much to do with the reviewer's assessment of how long it will take for these results to effect improvements in practice. Responses that imply the relative importance of the problem studied are significantly correlated with the time to effect impact for publication in either scientific and professional journals or HEW project reports. Presumably, for the Harvard reviewers, it is the relative importance of the problem rather than the source of the publication that determined the time lag.

The correlation analysis does imply that contributions to certain U.S. domestic health objectives are likely to effect improvements in a shorter length of time from publication in HEW reports, or, alternatively, that such results are more likely to be published in HEW reports. Thus, potential contributions to the objectives, morbidity reduction, promotion of positive health life, and solutions to environmental problems are more significantly correlated with the time to effect impact if published only in HEW reports than if published in scientific or professional journals.

Finally, the reviewer's confidence is significantly correlated with his responses concerning reasonable progress, proposed benefits, and actual project accomplishments. On balance, whatever the individual reviewer's criteria for reasonable progress may be, he has more confidence in his responses when the criteria are met.

Further Analysis of the Questionnaire Responses—Uncoded Comments

Many of the Harvard reviewers provided commentary upon their questionnaire responses and gave appraisals and analyses of the projects in addition to their coded responses. Some of the negative statements on project progress have been organized in order to find causal links among the projects that proved disappointing. The intent in presenting these is to provide information that may prove useful for the future operations of the program, rather than to castigate specific projects that may even be too far along to benefit from such advice. Thus, the information is presented without reference to the specific projects. In each case there is a brief discussion of the general and specific nature of the problem and, where relevant, a specific recommendation.

Lack of Contribution Toward U.S. Health Objectives

On fifteen of the projects, the reviewers expressed serious doubts as to whether the projects ever had any potential for making contributions to the U.S. domestic health objectives. A number of reasons were cited:

1. The disease or condition studied was of negligible proportions in the U.S.;

2. The organization and manpower allocations of the U.S. medical care delivery system rendered the findings inapplicable to the U.S.;

3. The characteristics and habits of the U.S. population were sufficiently different from those of the Yugoslav population groups studied that the project results could not be used in the U.S.; and

4. The disease or condition is widespread and so well studied in the U.S. and elsewhere that the findings of the projects are unlikely to contribute any valuable information to the U.S.

In some cases the reviewers excused the projects on the ground that the project results might be applicable to Americans of Balkan descent. In some instances such reasoning is patently specious, while in others there is minimal chance of the research results being passed on to the ultimate benefits of the American patient.

The Harvard evaluation team has the distinct impression that the workings of the HEW Special Foreign Currency Program project review processes are sufficiently designed to take into account the consideration of applicability to the United States. Unfortunately several projects have been funded that seemed at the time of their approval quite evidently to lack potential benefits to the U.S. The review bodies must have been able to perceive this, yet the projects were funded nevertheless. It is recommended that OIH examine cases in which the requirement that projects be beneficial to both countries is flouted. It should use its influence with the agency program heads to prevent the funding of new projects that ignore the health needs of the U.S.

Data Analysis Difficulties

The reviewers of several projects criticized the data-processing techniques of the research team. In many instances cost overruns were incurred to provide for data processing. On a smaller number of projects preparation for the organization and treatment of the data were praised. On still other projects the data handling difficulties were anticipated at the review stage and adequate preparations were arranged.

Program personnel in the agencies seem generally aware of the kinds of problems associated with data handling. It is recommended, however, that agency program heads and review sections give particular attention to the data-processing question, and institute a mechanism designed to identify the occasional project that has not foreseen or prepared for its data-processing needs.

Unpromising Research

The reviewers felt that the research promised by some proposals did not merit funding with Special Foreign Currency Program monies. They posited a number of reasons that should have been sufficient to disapprove the projects at the level of the scientific peer review:

1. Seven projects were felt to represent unprofitable duplication of previous research;

2. On three projects, the reviewers felt that the proposals envisioned expensive modes of obtaining information that were more cheaply available through other types of projects;

3. On nine projects, it was felt that the research plans laid out in the proposals outlined uninteresting and unpromising research directions. One of the projects cited for duplication fell into this category, but the majority were projects that the reviewers felt provided information that would not have high value to anyone. A smaller number of projects were taken to task for not approaching the research in the way deemed most likely to yield the desired results; and

4. The reviewers felt that the quality of presentation, documentation, and planning for four projects was so low that they ought not to have been approved.

It is difficult for study sections to correct errors of this type. They can reject the proposals with constructive suggestions for improvement, but this is a cumbersome process. Too often, however, the objections raised by study sections were ignored and the proposals approved without change. Perhaps this is because the proposals were actively solicited and the agencies therefore found it difficult to reject them. It is recommended that the project officers provide more assistance to the principal investigators in planning the research. Further, it is recommended that there be a systematic check instituted to assess the extent to which the review opinions of consulted American scientists are heeded.

Problems of the Contract Process

The reviewers found inherent difficulties in the procedures by which the research is agreed upon and funded. It is difficult to predict years in advance the exact best path for the future research to follow. After two years of a three-year contract, the researcher will know better what ought to be done in the third year than he did when he wrote the proposal. Several points related to the difficulty inherent in tying research to a present design were noted by the reviewers:

1. The problem is exacerbated when it takes a long time for the proposal to be approved;

2. Some researchers have simply failed to follow the agreed-upon protocol;

3. Applicants for the counterpart currencies see that they will have a better chance of success if they present an extremely ambitious research plan, many of which are impossible to fulfill;

4. Instances have been found in which the research envisioned in the protocol achieved publication before the official starting date for the project.

All of these problems are inherent in a system that funds research projects upon the basis of an application process. The problems would be lessened if the project approval process were more rapid and the monitoring role more systematic, but they would not be eliminated. It is recommended, however, that consideration be given to providing for more rapid review, and that a general provision be established for more systematic monitoring of projects by the project officers.

An Assessment of the Role of the Project Officer

A project officer—referred to in earlier agreements as a program officer—is charged with overall responsibility for the administration of each grant agreement. This responsibility, which is exercised on behalf of the granting agency of the United States government, is intended to match that of the principal investigator in Yugoslavia, who is responsible for "active direction" of the project and for its administration on behalf of the Yugoslav institution to which the grant is made.

The standard research grant agreement also includes the following references to the project officer:

"Since the course of any scientific investigation is not entirely predictable . . . a change in approach or technique used may be made after appropriate consultations between the . . . Principal Investigator and the Project Officer.

Any circumstances which in the opinion of the Principal Investigator or the collaborating institution will require a modification of more than 10% from each of the estimated items of expenditure will require prior approval of the Project Officer.

None of the arrangements for reports shall preclude full informational exchange of correspondence or other communication between the Principal Investigator and the Project Officer.

Officers or employees of the Yugoslav Collaborating Institution or other personnel assigned to or engaged in the conduct of this project shall be available for consultation with the Project Officer or his representative at any reasonable time.

Changes or substitution of Principal Investigator will be made only with written approval from the Project Officer."

Although it is not explicitly so stated on the agreement, it is assumed that the project officer will also exercise the other rights of the granting agency, including:

1. Making arrangements for periodic payments in local currency of the specified amounts;

2. Providing expert consultants as needed;

3. Assisting in the arrangements for any agreed-upon travel to the United States by the principal investigator or his collaborators;

4. Receiving and reviewing the required progress reports of the scientific aspects of the research;

5. Receiving and reviewing the annual fiscal reports; and

6. Recommending the authorization of payments for each succeeding period of the agreement after evaluating the information about estimated future requirements provided by the principal investigator.

It is also assumed that the project officer will exercise on behalf of the United States granting agency the right of access to facilities, records, and accounts "for the purpose of observing the status and progress of the project." Budgetary provision is therefore included in the project agreement for the travel costs involved.

It is clear that the intention was to assign to the project officer an important role in the execution of the research agreement. Albeit few of the projects have been concluded, some general remarks, tentative conclusions, and recommendations can be made about the performance of the project officers, based on conversations with selected project officers, and on the trip reports that are made after each journey to Yugoslavia. The impressions of members of the Yugoslav evaluation team and of several Yugoslav principal investigators have also been taken into account.

Appointment of Project Officer

The United States granting agency appears to have complete freedom of choice in the selection of project officers. The majority of project officers are staff members of the granting agencies, but a significant number are recruited from universities and a few from other institutions. (The distribution of project officers by primary locus of responsibility is outlined in Table 4-19.) Among the agencies, NIH displays the highest propensity to recruit project officers from outside the agency. In part, this may be related to the nature of the research sponsored by NIH, but it may also reflect a different policy at NIH concerning the role of the project officer and the importance of recruiting project officers with particular expertise relative to the research area of the specific projects.

There is a significant difference in the number of projects supervised by a project officer. (The distribution of the number of projects supervised by project officers is outlined in Table 4-20.) Sixty-seven project officers were responsible for only one project. The remaining forty-three projects were divided among only twelve project officers. At the extreme, one project officer was responsible for seven projects, and one for eight. Clearly, either the relative proportion of one's time devoted to the role of project officer is quite different among them, or the role they play is quite different.

Table 4-19
Distribution of Project Officers by Primary Locus of Responsibility

Locus	Number
Department of Health, Education, and Welfare	
NIH	14
HSMHA	58
FDA	6
EPA	1
OIH	1
Universities	22
Clinics and hospitals	5
Research institutes	2
State health departments	1
Total	110

Table 4-20
Distribution of Projects Supervised Per Project Officer

Number of Projects Supervised	Number of Project Officers
1	67
2	5
3	2
4	3
5	0
6	0
7	1
8	1

In this general context, three recommendations seem to be in order. First, care should be taken to appoint as project officers only individuals who by their scientific training and research experience can understand all aspects of the research project and give substantial assistance at all stages, particularly in the preparation of the research protocol, in budgeting, in preparing requests for amendments, and in the publication of research papers in scientific journals. Second, if for any reason a project officer is appointed who does not have the prescribed training and experience, a consultant should be appointed who will give professional assistance as required. Third, the role of the project officer should be more fully described in the agreement and the tasks that he should perform at each stage of the project specified.

Project Initiation

Several of the project officers apparently played an important part in interesting Yugoslav investigators in a problem which both then developed into a project. In some cases the Yugoslav scientists had already worked in the same laboratory as the project officer in the United States and the project was developed as a continuation of the U.S. research. In such cases the project officer gave considerable assistance in drafting the project proposal, obtaining favorable reviews of the proposal, and getting the project awarded.

In other cases the project officer appears to have been chosen only because he was a staff member of the agency. There is no evidence in such cases that the project received any special assistance from the project officer, who seems to play only a passive administrative role of receiving reports.

Trip Reports

Project officers are apparently required to submit a report for each journey overseas. These trip reports are potential sources of information on the status of the projects supervised by the reporting officer. The actual value of these reports as sources of information, however, ranges from very little to quite considerable. In some cases all that is recorded is the date of the journey, the places visited, and the persons met, embellished with personal comments about places and persons but no substantial information about the actual status of the project. Other project officers report in detail the discussions held with the principal investigators, the problems confronting the project, and the steps proposed for solving them.

Some trip reports deal with a visit concerned only with a single project, while others combine several projects and other travel, with an attendance at a conference and visits to other countries.

It is strongly recommended that a policy be established requiring that trip reports should uniformly deal with every aspect of the project—progress to date, problems that have arisen, status of supplies and equipment, results already achieved, and proposals, if any, for amendments of the original agreement.

Project Monitoring

Although this would appear to be the principal continuing role of the project officer, in the vast majority of cases there is no evidence in the available files that the project officer had any contact with the principal investigator between visits, either by correspondence or by other methods of communication. Several project officers responded when asked for information by members of the evaluation team that they were either waiting for a progress report or had heard nothing from the project staff since the previous visit.

Many projects have been amended, some a number of times. Information concerning how the amendments were made is uniformly scanty as far as the development of the necessity for amendment is concerned. Apart from claiming increased costs, or the results of devaluation of the Yugoslav currency, or salary revisions necessitated by statutory regulations, there is no supporting correspondence, and there is no evidence that the project officer was consulted as required by the project agreement.

Three recommendations are in order concerning project monitoring. The project officer should be required to report at least once a year on the progress of the project. Such reports should complement, not replace, the trip reports made after each visit to the project, and should summarize developments of the project and record all decisions made by the project officer. The opinions of the project officer should be recorded on each item of any proposed amendment to the agreement. The views of any consultant and of the original review team should also be obtained and kept in the record. Finally, all correspondence between the principal investigator and the project officer should be included in the master file of each project, in order to provide the background for all decisions taken by the project officer in carrying out his duties relating to the project.

Publications

Until special enquiries were made by the Harvard evaluation team, the record of publications, especially in English, was very scanty. (In order to gain some perspective on the extent to which research results are in fact published, the Yugoslav evaluation team was asked to provide a listing of the publications that have appeared to date or are scheduled to appear in scientific or professional journals. The information they provided is summarized in Table A-5 in the Appendix.) Moreover, even for those projects for which there were reports that appear to be suitable for publication, there is no evidence that anything was done to secure such publication and to bring the reports to the attention of American scientists in the same field. This should be one of the principal duties of the project officer, who is often in a better position to accomplish this than the principal investigator.

It is strongly recommended that the project officer should be made responsible for ensuring appropriate publication of reports of the research done in each project.

The Project Officer and Program Impact

Given the small number of projects actually completed, it is not possible to have any final conclusions on the role of the project officer and the extent to which it affected the impact of the program. The nature of the program and the significant difference that a project officer can make, however, confirm the impression that more interested participation in project initiation, more continuous project monitoring, and more complete reporting of progress would contribute toward a higher performance for most projects.

Amendments and Cost Overruns

It is perhaps appropriate to conclude the general evaluation of the Special Foreign Currency Program in Yugoslavia with a brief discussion of the related phenomena of amendments and cost overruns. A significant number of the projects have been amended to incorporate budget increases.

The extent to which this program is characterized by amendments to projects is reflected in Table 4-21, which outlines the number of projects amended and the number of subsequent amendments according to the year in which the projects in question were originally funded. Through 1970, 59 projects had been initiated, and no less than 46 of these have been amended. Among the 46

Table 4-21

Summary of Project Amendments by Year of Initial Project Funding

Year of Initial Funding	Number of Projects Originally Funded	Number of Projects Amended	Number of Amendments
1960	1	1	7
1961	0	0	0
1962	1	1	1
1963	1	1	3
1964	3	2	10
1965	3	3	6
1966	3	3	9
1967	7	6	12
1968	15	12	23
1969	17	12	18
1970	8	5	5
1971	49	3	6
1972	2	0	0

projects amended, 34 were HSMHA projects, 9 were NIH projects, and 3 were FDA projects. Since the agencies had funded 43, 12, and 3 projects respectively through 1970, it would appear that the propensity to amend is not unique to any agency. The number of projects amended and the number of amendments are summarized by agency in Table 4-22.

Of course, the fact that a project has been amended is not evidence of poor performance. In some cases project agreements were originally signed for a limited number of years, but with a clear indication that the agency intended to support the project for an additional period. In other cases, although amendments were probably not anticipated, they seemed justified and perhaps enhanced the potential impact of the program. In some cases, however, the amendments were probably not justified, and there is some evidence that poor projects, known to be poor and to have little potential impact, have been amended and continued.

Not all amendments involve significant budget increases, but most do. In order to define the problem, the Harvard evaluation team developed a criterion for identifying cost overruns. A project was classified as having incurred a significant cost overrun if its budget was increased by more than 50 percent or over $50,000. Thirty-two projects did have significant cost overruns by this criterion.

The reasons for cost overruns are quite varied. The actual reasons offered in the supporting material for requests for increased budgets run across a rather wide spectrum. Yet there is a pattern to the reasons. These reasons have been analyzed and they seem to fall into five major categories, as outlined in Table 4-23.

A review of the projects that have been amended to incorporate a significant cost overrun uncovered quite different case types. Some projects were originally

Table 4-22
Summary of Project Amendments by Agency

Number of Amendments	Number of Projects				
	NIH	HSMHA	FDA	EPA	Total
0	23	34	3	1	61
1	6	14	2	0	22
2	1	11	1	0	13
3	1	8	0	0	9
4	0	2	1	0	3
5	0	0	0	0	0
6	0	1	0	0	1
7	1	0	0	0	1
	32	70	7	1	110

Table 4-23
Summary of Reasons for Budget Increases

I. Extension of Project
   a. Continuation of original study (to accumulate more data and statistics to provide for better analysis/results/conclusions)
   b. Renewal of project (where original study was Phase I or pilot study and Phase II or follow-up study is proposed)
   c. Problems in gearing-up (recruiting personnel, establishing research center, defining sample group, delays in funding from Embassy)
   d. Inadequacies in original study design (poorly written original proposal, faulty methodology employed, irrelevant study goals, inexperienced staff)
   e. Translating, writing, printing final report (when not included in original agreement)
   f. Insufficient budget/time period for original study (project submitted several years before finally approved and therefore budget insufficient due to inflation, rising salaries/wages; or because financial and time needs of project underestimated in original agreement)
   g. Conference (when original project was a conference and amendment allows for a subsequent conference)

II. Expansion of Scope
   a. Modification in study design (new research techniques, increased testing/sampling)
   b. Expansion of study objectives (new areas of fruitful or necessary research discovered in course of doing original research work)
   c. Increase of study/sample group (enlarging the total sample group or replacement of one sample group by another due to disqualification; or, in case of fellowship program, increasing the number of student participants)
   d. Increase in personnel/staff
   e. Increase in equipment/services/materials
   f. Increased travel
   g. Conference or symposium (when project not originally scheduled to have a conference but does due to amendment)

III. Inflation
   a. Salaries/wages
   b. Equipment costs
   c. Overhead costs (utilities, rents, etc.)
   d. Services (subcontractors for computer analysis, translating, printing costs)
   e. Internal travel costs (when cost of travel allowed under original agreement increases)

IV. Devaluation
   a. Equipment (imported)
   b. International travel

V. Financial Audit
   (When not required under original agreement because project began before audit was requirement)

designed as and intended to be pilot studies. The amendment material indicates that a review and evaluation of the pilot study was undertaken and on the basis of the relative success of the pilot, the amendment provides for a further research effort. The use of pilot research efforts to determine feasibility is traditional and appropriate. Pilot studies should not be discouraged in programs such as the Special Foreign Currency Program in Yugoslavia. On the contrary, this evaluation study indicates that they should be employed far more often than they actually are.

In a number of cases the projects were not designed as a pilot study, but in practice turned out to be. Such research efforts, because of poor design, inadequate direction, and the like, involved a more or less shotgun approach in the original study. In the process, however, a feasible and useful research effort was identified. The purpose of the amendment was to allow for a new, more appropriately directed and concentrated research effort. The question to be raised in this context is not with the amendment, but rather with the funding of the original project. What should have been funded in the first instance was a pilot study. Again, time, effort, and money would often be better utilized if shorter, less expensive pilot studies preceded major full-scale research efforts.

Unfortunately there are cases that involve a major effort, perhaps the collection of a significant volume of data, but produce no real results. This may be due to poor research design, data problems, or a variety of factors. Whatever the cause noted, the amendments seem to argue that since so much money has been expended with no result, it is necessary to spend still more in order to salvage something. This is poor strategy, whether applied by a poor poker player or the supporters of research.

Why does a project continue to get funding if it does not display reasonable progress? It will be recalled that the reviewers ranked actual accomplishments somewhat lower than proposed objectives. Of course there are many factors that contribute to lower rankings for actual accomplishments, but some part of the lower ranking is undoubtedly due to lack of reasonable progress. In order to gain an additional perspective the reviewers were asked to answer two specific questions for all projects that had had a significant cost overrun. First, they were asked whether or not they would have approved funding the project initially if the actual cost had been known. Presumably they were assessing the proposed benefits in terms of the actual cost. In almost 20 percent of the cases their responses were negative. Albeit this is clearly hindsight, it does suggest that more concern should be given to the eventual cost of a project when it is first considered. Second, they were asked whether or not they considered the amendment justified. In effect they were asked to assess the actual accomplishments in terms of the actual cost. In approximately 25 percent of the cases their responses were negative. This is not hindsight, and suggests that many projects continue to get funding that should be terminated.

Why does a project continue to get funding if it does not display reasonable progress? Undoubtedly a number of factors contribute. There is, of course, the poor-strategy phenomenon mentioned above. Determining when to cut one's losses is often difficult. More often than not, however, the confounding issue is that of sunk costs. The decision to spend additional funds must be based on the expected return from the additional funds. It is just not appropriate to justify additional funds on the ground that so much has already been spent that something has to be salvaged.

Two additional factors are particularly relevant to the decision-makers in the context of this program. First, project officers and other agency personnel have often engaged in active solicitation of proposals. There is an understandable reluctance to terminate research that may have been initiated in large part because the agency personnel suggested it to Yugoslav officials or researchers, or both. Second, given the process by which the relative shares of the several agencies are determined, there is an incentive for each agency to continue to support existing projects.

5

Some Special In-Depth Analyses

Introduction

The two previous chapters have been devoted to analyses of the Special Foreign Currency Program in Yugoslavia in general. The overview of the program outlined in Chapter 3 included a general analysis of the types of research or major activities undertaken by the 110 projects and concentrated on the trends in the size and scope of the general program over time. Chapter 4 involved essentially an analysis of the project reviews as a basis for a general evaluation of the potential impact of the program. This chapter is devoted to a number of special in-depth analyses of certain aspects of the program.

The Special Foreign Currency Program in Yugoslavia in fact is overwhelmingly a recent program. Of the 110 projects reviewed, 51 had not started by the first of 1971. More significant, 95 of the projects were not scheduled to be completed by the end of 1971. Thus, in most cases the evaluation teams had to make projections of potential impact rather than attempt to measure actual impact. Since evaluation should be designed to marshal information that will serve the purpose of improving decisions, the fact that a major proportion of program activity presumably is subject to future decisions may enhance the usefulness of the assessment of potential impact that is the basis of most of this report. On the other hand, it is important to assess actual impact in those cases where it is feasible, however few. Hence, a concentrated effort was undertaken to assess the impact of a number of completed projects. This special in-depth analysis is outlined in the next section.

Laboratory research, clinical research, epidemiological research, and combinations of these are the major activity of the majority of the 110 projects. Yet approximately a quarter of the projects of the program involve quite different and somewhat unique activities. In order to fully understand the program it is necessary to take a careful look at these other activities and an attempt has been made to assess their potential impact separately. Special in-depth analyses are outlined below for student exchange programs, conferences, translations, and critical reviews of literature.

The Impact of Completed Projects

The impact of nine completed projects has been assessed. As with each of the 110 projects, each completed project has been reviewed at least twice by the

Harvard reviewers, but in addition, information has been obtained from a number of experts or specialists in the fields most related to the research effort of each project. Additional information was sought from specialists in the field of the project research for two reasons. First, their assessment as experts in the field would serve to complement the assessments of the Harvard reviewers. Second, and more important, since the impact of research efforts in Yugoslavia upon the United States clearly requires appropriate dissemination of the results, it was important to determine the extent to which the projects and their results were known to U.S. experts in the relevant fields.

For each of the projects, the names of five to seven specialists who should be familiar with the subject studied were selected. Two separate interviews were held with each expert. After the reason for the survey was explained, they were given the title of the project, the name of the project director in Yugoslavia, and the name of the U.S. project officer. They were asked immediately if they knew of this work done in Yugoslavia, and their answer was recorded as: "Yes," "No," or "Vaguely." Each specialist, including those who answered "Yes," was given the same information about the project, including the general scope, outline, and a summary of the general results. They were also given references to publications. Finally, they were asked if they would be willing to review the material given to them and undergo a second interview.

During the second interview they were asked two specific questions: if "the project reliably executed and sufficiently publicized" was in their opinion of maximal, great, some, small, or no benefit to the United States; and if as a member of a support distributing group they would "consider, depending on more careful scrutiny of the application, to support this project." The answer to the second question was recorded as "Yes," "No," or "Doubtful." The responses of the specialists are summarized in Table 5-1. The responses of the Harvard reviewers for proposed benefits relative to budget allocated, the actual project accomplishments relative to budget allocated, and the specific advantages of implementing the project in Yugoslavia are outlined for the same nine completed projects in Table 5-2.

1. Study of the Epidemiology of Cardiovascular Diseases and Social Change

Data from this work were presented at eleven conferences and seminars; all presentations were to an international audience. Two well-read articles have so far appeared in American journals, four in Yugoslav journals, and chapters in three textbooks were based on this study.

The project officer was deeply involved in this project. He and his staff visited the project frequently, and have stimulated and participated in the preparation of manuscripts.

Table 5-1

Summary of Specialists' Responses for Nine Completed Projects

Project	Number of Specialists Contacted	Knew of This Project			Benefit to the U.S.						Would Support This Project			
		Yes	No	Vaguely	Maximal	Great	Some	Small	No	NA[a]	Yes	No	Doubtful	NA[a]
1. Epidemiology of cardiovascular diseases and social change	6	4	2	0	1	2	2	0	0	1	4	0	1	1
2. } 3. } Infant genetic disorders	5	3	2	0	0	4	0	1	0	0	4	1	0	0
4. Child mortality	5	1	4	0	0	0	1	3	1	0	1	4	0	0
5. } 6. } Organization of health care delivery I & II	6	5	0	1	1	3	1	0	0	1	4	0	1	1
7. Family planning and limitation	5	2	3	0	1	3	0	1	0	0	4	1	0	0
8. Mental illness	6	3	2	1	1	2	1	1	0	1	3	1	1	1
9. Training for family (comprehensive-primary) care	7	3	2	2	1	2	2	0	1	1	3	2	1	1
	40	21	15	4	5	16	7	6	2	4	23	9	4	4

[a]Not available for second interview.

Table 5-2

Summary of Harvard Reviewers' Responses to Proposed Objectives, Actual Accomplishments, and Specific Advantage of Yugoslavia for Nine Completed Projects

Project	Average Response by Project		
	Rating of Proposed Project Objectives	Rating of Actual Project Accomplishments	Rating of Specific Advantages of Implementation in Yugoslavia
1. Epidemiology of cardiovascular diseases and social change	2.0	2.0	2.0
2. Infant genetic disorders	2.5	3.0	3.0
3. Infant genetic disorders	2.5	3.0	3.0
4. Child mortality	1.5	4.0	2.0
5. Organization of health care delivery I	2.0	2.5	2.5
6. Organization of health care delivery II	1.5	2.5	2.5
7. Family planning and limitation	2.0	1.5	1.5
8. Mental illness	2.5	3.0	2.5
9. Training for family (comprehensive-primary) care	2.0	2.0	1.7

Key to ratings: 1. Maximal benefit or advantage
2. Great benefit or advantage
3. Some benefit or advantage
4. Small benefit or advantage
5. No benefit or advantage

The carefully collected data on patient populations are now being used in a new project.

The final report, written jointly by Yugoslav and U.S. investigators, should have considerable additional impact.

This project demonstrates the great contribution a dedicated, interested, and scientifically competent project officer can make, even though the project officer himself stated in an interview that he "could not devote as much time as warranted and advantageous."

This project was well known by U.S. specialists, who considered it to be of great importance to the scientific progress and to better health care in the U.S. (see Table 5-1). The two Harvard reviewers of this project also gave the project a high rating (see Table 5-2).

2. A Study of Infant Genetic Disorders

This project is inseparable from and overlaps number 3, which used the same cases, methods, and personnel. They will therefore be discussed together.

3. Follow-up on Infant Genetic Disorders

The subject of these two projects is not a very frequent condition, but is very important because the dramatic pathological consequences are fully preventable when the disease is detected early.

Results from these studies have been presented and discussed at several international meetings. As far as could be determined, only one paper was written and published in a Yugoslav journal, but the project officer who took over when the original officer retired in 1972 gave assurance that several papers are in progress. The project officer always involved a number of other scientists in his activities. The officer was able to find funding to send numerous collaborators to Yugoslavia and to the many other countries where he was also involved. This accounts for the fact that his projects were well known and discussed even without many publications (see Table 5-1).

Perhaps due to the low frequency of the condition studied, the two Harvard reviewers, who were not specialists in either pediatrics or genetic diseases, rated both projects relatively low (see Table 5-2).

4. Factors in Child Mortality

It seems that an enormous amount of data has been collected by numerous people who now have difficulty getting together to write either a final report or other publications. The project officer confirmed that the task is "almost impossible." Several methodological manuals have been written and are being used by other investigators. As one reviewer of the Harvard evaluation team states, "the investigators seem to have gotten lost in the methodology" and "an extensive analysis has been performed with little elucidation." If the data are made usable, the results from this project could be of great value to the decision-makers in the Yugoslav health care system, but it is questionable if they would be of value anywhere else.

Except for one, the U.S. specialists in epidemiology and biostatistics were not aware of this work being done in Yugoslavia. When it was described, they did not seem to understand how the results could benefit the U.S. and how any conclusions could be applied anywhere except in Yugoslavia (see Table 5-1).

The two Harvard reviewers, probably interpreting the question as "advantages for Yugoslavia," rated the advantages of implementing this study in Yugoslavia as great. They rated the proposed benefits of project in relation to the budget allocated considerably higher than the actual accomplishments, indicating some disappointment with the results (see Table 5-2).

5. Study of the Organization of Health Care Delivery I

The purpose of this study was to develop techniques for measuring and evaluating the use of medical care by populations. In this sense it was really a pilot study and under WHO sponsorship has been extended to a number of countries. The greatest impact of this work was outside Yugoslavia, particularly in those countries in which these studies are now underway.

The two Harvard reviewers gave this project relatively high ratings, apparently in recognition of its value as preparatory work (see Table 5-2).

The full-scale study in Yugoslavia was supported by forming the following project:

6. Study of the Organization of Health Care Delivery II

This project, as part of a worldwide study, is well known and has been widely discussed.

Data from the work in Yugoslavia have been used at many conferences and seminars. A publication in book form is in preparation. Some of the results have been published in a Department of Health, Education, and Welfare series.

There can no question of the considerable impact this project has had internationally. This is implicit in the responses of the specialists (Table 5-1), and the high rating given by the Harvard reviewers (see Table 5-2).

7. Study of Family Planning and Limitation

This project was very well designed and planned, but unfortunately it ran into an unforeseen and unavoidable difficulty. At the beginning of the study, abortion was freely available and widely used in Yugoslavia, while contraceptive services were difficult to obtain. Simultaneously with this project and, as some feel, partly as a consequence, contraception in Yugoslavia was legalized and made available to the whole population. This all but destroyed the control group of abortions (without available contraceptives). Nevertheless, the study "indicated" that with an effective contraceptive program the abortion rate becomes negligible. Without control groups (and with poor statistical evaluation) the reports are inadequate, and there have been no publications.

The project officer involved several colleagues in this study, and one in particular has collaborated very actively and has given talks on the singular success of this program.

Consequently, even with the absence of publication, this project was moderately well known by other specialists in the field and considered very important in view of the magnitude of the worldwide problem of abortion vs. contraception (Table 5-1).

The Harvard reviewers, apparently for the same reason, also rated this project quite high (Table 5-2).

8. A Study of Mental Illness

This project is actually the continuation—or perhaps conclusion—of a much longer study, of at least ten years' duration, funded from different sources. Only the last three years were financed under the Special Foreign Currency Program. In 1951, the project officer did a survey in Yugoslavia on the subject, and since that time has spent almost six weeks in Yugoslavia every summer.

Data from this study have been contributed to many international meetings, and at least sixteen Yugoslav and two American publications are listed for the period before Special Foreign Currency Program support began. Since that time, three articles have appeared in an important American publication.

The driving force in this project was clearly the U.S. project officer, who feels that he created in Yugoslavia an interest and capability to conduct studies in psychiatric epidemiology. He also played an important part in the planning of the study and in the writing of papers and the final report.

This project has stimulated further ongoing studies in this field in Yugoslavia and other parts of the world. It is known and recognized by a number of specialists in spite of the relatively low popularity of psychiatric epidemiology (Table 5-1). The Harvard reviewers rated this project between some and great benefit (Table 5-2).

9. A Study Evaluating the Training for Family
(Comprehensive-Primary) Care

This project was intended as a two-year pilot study to precede a full-scale investigation of the possible "specialization" of general practitioners, without the inherent danger and disadvantage of turning the G.P.s into real specialists of curative medicine. This is obviously a subject of great importance to all countries and, as far as is known, not explored anywhere else. Unfortunately, funding for the full-scale study was not obtained, so that work on this subject was not continued.

Nevertheless, the data obtained in this exploratory study are convincing and important enough to be used, reported, and discussed by many specialists concerned with health care delivery. Some of the findings have been incorporated into a book. A xeroxed report is widely circulated and has stimulated a researcher in another country to embark on a closely related and similar project.

Unfortunately, the project officer retired at a very critical time. The project was turned over to a professional at HSMHA who did not have great experience in this field, had never visited Yugoslavia, and did not know the Yugoslav investigators. The new project officer has a two-volume report on this exploratory study, but is not in a position to stimulate publication of this report or part of it, which clearly would be of critical importance at this stage to encourage further funding. The new project officer plans to go to Yugoslavia and salvage material for publication in the U.S.; a plan which certainly should be vigorously supported. So far, there are only two articles published in Serbo-Croatian and a report in a major American newspaper.

The majority of specialists in health care planning in one way or another heard about this project and thought that its purpose was extremely important (Table 5-1). The Harvard reviewers also rated this project very highly (Table 5-2).

Any attempt to identify the impact of a project in the health field must take into account the fact that results of such studies usually take a reasonably long time to be recognized and even more time to be implemented. Quite often, before implementation on the practical health care delivery level, it is necessary to re-evaluate the results under various conditions. When considered in this appropriate context, the fact that most of these Yugoslav projects were usually well known by more than half the specialists in the various fields, that most of the specialists considered most projects as possessing considerable benefit for the U.S., and that many of them would have been in favor of supporting most of the projects augurs well for the potential impact on the U.S. of the Special Foreign Currency Program.

On balance, it would appear that most of these nine completed projects have begun to have some impact on the United States. In seven of the nine cases, more specialists knew of the project than not. Given that in many cases there were not a significant number of publications, this is perhaps encouraging. Further, in eight of the nine cases the specialists would appear to have rather high opinions concerning the projects.

Still, almost half of the specialists (fifteen) either did not know of the project or were only vaguely aware of it (four), even though the subject was in their special field of interest. The stimulation of and assistance in writing more well-read publications still seem to be neglected aspects of the U.S. collaboration and should be emphasized as obligations of the project officers.

Student Exchange Programs

Actually, "student exchange" is a misnomer. There are not exchange programs, but rather public health fellowship programs which provide for students from U.S. medical schools to spend time in Yugoslavia. During the first three and one-half years of this Special-Foreign-Currency-Program-supported fellowship program (until the end of 1972), 152 students from 57 U.S. medical schools spent ten to twelve weeks in Yugoslavia. Fifty-two students participated in programs at the Faculty of Medicine in Belgrade, 28 students at the School of Public Health in Belgrade, and 72 students at the Andrija Stampar School of Public Health in Zagreb.

U.S. medical schools did not have balanced representation in this program. This might have been due to either the advertising of the program or the selection process in the U.S. More than 10 percent (16 students) came from one medical school (Harvard), more than 20 percent (33 students) came from three medical schools (Harvard, University of California in San Francisco, and the University of Pennsylvania), and more than 50 percent (77 students) came from twelve medical schools.

By July 1972, 106 students had completed their fellowships. At this point, approximately one-half of the programed time was passed. Given the total budget of some $650,000, the cost per student for ten to twelve weeks was approximately $3000.

In order to gain some insight to the impact of this fellowship program on the participants, a questionnaire was designed to gather relevant information. This questionnaire was mailed to each of the 106 medical students who had participated in the program. (A copy of the questionnaire is included in the appendix.) The response for this questionnaire was exceptionally good. Ninety-three completed questionnaires, a response rate of 87 percent, were returned.

Eighty-seven percent of the respondents were men and 13 percent were women. One-third of the participants were married. Response to the questions provides considerable insight into the impact of the fellowship program. A list of reasons for applying to the program was provided, and respondents were asked to check one or more such reasons. Almost all of them listed "study of a different health care system" as one of the reasons; 83 percent checked the "desire to live and learn from a different society and culture," a little more than half checked "study of disease and health conditions different from those in the U.S." and 43 percent checked also "the desire to get away from U.S. medical school routine."

The participants were then asked to evaluate the briefing they received in the United States and in Yugoslavia. Less than 10 percent of the participants judged the briefing received in the U.S. as either very good or good. Thirty-eight percent judged the briefing as acceptable, and 18 percent as nonacceptable. More than one-third of the participants indicated they had received *no* briefing in the U.S. By contrast, the briefing received in Yugoslavia was judged much better. First, *all* respondents indicated they had been briefed in Yugoslavia, and almost 80 percent said that the briefing had either been very good (38 percent) or good (39 percent); only 18 percent judged the briefing as merely acceptable, and 5 percent as nonacceptable.

More than half of the respondents judged living arrangements in Yugoslavia as either very good (29 percent) or good (24 percent); one-third replied that these arrangements were acceptable, and 14 percent that they were nonacceptable.

Relationships to Yugoslav preceptors and other faculty and professional staff were rated overwhelmingly as very good (53 percent) or good (32 percent), and only 3 percent judged such relationships as nonacceptable. This confirms other evidence that the Yugoslavs have gone out of their way to make the stay of American medical students a meaningful and pleasant experience. By the same token, relationships with Yugoslav costudents were even better than with staff, with 90 percent of the respondents checking either very good (66 percent) or good (24 percent), and only 10 percent acceptable.

The relationships of the students with Yugoslav administrators of the program also came out quite favorably. Eighty-three percent of the students judged these relationships as either very good (41 percent) or good (42 percent), and only 5 percent as nonacceptable.

It might have been predicted that language knowledge or lack thereof would be an important element in the experience of the students. The majority of the students had no knowledge of Serbo-Croatian (77 percent), while only 6 percent spoke it moderately well and 11 percent a little. And yet lack of language knowledge or proficiency was not seen as a serious impediment. Indeed, only 6 percent of the respondents indicated as much, though 60 percent said it was some impediment. One-third of the respondents answered that the lack of language knowledge presented either little or no impediment.

In terms of their activities in Yugoslavia, the overwhelming majority did projects in preventive medicine/public health and community health (83 percent) and 13 percent concentrated in curative medicine. Only 2 percent were engaged in basic sciences.

According to the students, activities in Yugoslavia changed or influenced the career plans of 44 percent, and did not change those of 45 percent. (Eleven percent did not respond.)

The most frequent change in career plans indicated by the participants was toward preventive medicine and public health. For example, out of 52 students who before going to Yugoslavia had planned to go into clinical curative medicine, 8, or 16 percent, now plan a career in public health. Even for most of those students whose career plans have not changed, their "general outlook on medical care changed"; they now realize "the importance of health planning" (13 students), the "importance of social medicine and of a national health care system" (15 students), the "general importance of preventive medicine" (4 students), and became "more critical of the U.S. health care system" (8 students), and of "socialized medicine in Yugoslavia" (2 students). Many students (22) simply stated that their attitude had changed, but did not elaborate. There is therefore little doubt that the exposure of American medical students to a foreign medical or health care system had a significant impact on their career planning and perception of medicine as a "public service."

The respondents were then asked to single out their "most important *medical* experience in Yugoslavia." The results were as follows:

- 30% The visit to rural health centers
- 28% The contact with Yugoslav diseases and their methods of coping with them
- 18% Recognizing the importance of preventive medicine and health care planning
- 11% Meeting Yugoslav medical experts
- 4% Contact with Yugoslav and U.S. participants

The single most important *nonmedical* experience in Yugoslavia was:

- 48% Contact with Yugoslav people and culture
- 31% Tourism
- 17% Meeting Yugoslav medical students
- 2% Visiting relatives
- 2% Meeting future spouse

Altogether, 61 percent rated their nonmedical experience as more significant, 22 percent found their medical and nonmedical experiences equally significant. Only 17 percent rated the medical experience as more significant.

Half of the participants found the experience in Yugoslavia much better than expected and an additional 21 percent better than expected; 21 percent rated their experience as "about as expected" and only 5 percent as "less valuable than expected." Further, for married students, 60 percent of the spouses found the Yugoslav experience "much better than expected," 24 percent "better than expected," and 4 percent "about as expected."

On balance, the U.S. medical students had a very high opinion of the program as a whole, apparently more for sociocultural than medical-academic reasons, even though 94 percent entered the program to "study a different health care system." The strong public health orientation in Yugoslavia clearly left its mark on the students, changing both their attitude towards health care delivery systems and, for some, even their career choices.

In future programs, whether in Yugoslavia or elsewhere, more attention should be given to and a better method found for the briefing of the students *before* they embark for a foreign country. This is particularly important if the program takes place in a country that does not have the facilities and manpower for the excellent briefing, supervision, and preceptorship these students apparently had in Yugoslavia. Many students also complained about the lack of follow-up after they returned to the U.S. Even though 88 percent of the students did write reports on their activities, either to the Association of American Medical Colleges (22 students), the Yugoslav project director (45 students), or to their own medical school advisor (12 students), only 6 reports were printed in any form and most of them were not distributed at all. The students surveyed expressed an interest in seminars, round-table discussions, and lectures prior to leaving for Yugoslavia, and perhaps a follow-up meeting for the participants after their return.

In their "remarks," the students expressed a great deal of concern about the selection process for this program. Many felt that the large Eastern and California schools have an advantage, and that motivation, though difficult to measure, should be considered more than academic excellence.

Many said that they are embarrassed by the lack of reciprocity of this program, which in Yugoslavia is known as an "Exchange Program." Only a relatively small ($60,000) program for "Postgraduate Medical Fellowships for Yugoslav Physicians" was started two years ago and can therefore not yet be evaluated. The students felt strongly that their Yugoslav student colleagues should have an opportunity to come to the U.S., and some of them have made such arrangements with their own universities.

Some students complained about the "inflation in Yugoslavia," and thereby insufficient funds, but others said that the financial support is clearly sufficient; a few said that the support is overly generous compared to the standard of living for Yugoslav medical students.

On the issue of language training, all felt that "a few words" would be helpful, but the majority seemed to believe that intensive training in Serbo-Croatian would not be worthwhile in view of the many other pressing needs (including other more "useful" languages) of the medical school curriculum.

During the Harvard evaluation team's visits to Yugoslavia, the project directors and a few other Yugoslavs involved in the "Student Programs" were interviewed. Although some of them expressed certain misgivings about the programs, they all, in principle, looked at the programs as a very important and highly desirable component of the Special Foreign Currency Program in Yugoslavia. They outlined advantages and disadvantages, with the advantages outweighing the disadvantages. The following are quotes from these interviews:

Advantages

The Yugoslavs would even try to fund this program with Yugoslav money, if no U.S. money available, because it is intellectually enriching to Yugoslav students and faculty.

Yugoslav students stimulated to think about community health.

Adds prestige to community health.

Improves relationships with Western countries and scientists, broadening views.

Disadvantages

Yugoslav students feel pushed aside.

More Serbo-Croatian language facility needed.

Research programs should be more carefully chosen and students should come prepared to work on them.

There should be a reciprocal program for Yugoslav students in U.S. to maintain good will.

Stimulation to Yugoslav-U.S. brain drain.

Six Harvard reviewers answered the questionnaires for project review for the three "Fellowship Programs for Students from U.S. Medical Schools." Each reported great benefit in relation to the amount of money allocated, both for proposed project objectives and for actual project accomplishments. They rated the implementation in Yugoslavia as being of maximal advantage. Some of their uncoded comments are informative: "Maximal advantage of implementation in Yugoslavia." "Very valuable because it breaks down the parochialism of American medical students." "May provide useful suggestions, insights for altering the U.S. health service delivery system." "Very impressed with quality of research projects."

In summary, there can be no question that these three Student Fellowship Programs, with a combined budget of approximately $650,000—less than 3 percent of the total budget to date of the Special Foreign Currency Program—did have a highly beneficial impact on the international activities of U.S. medical schools, and are very popular with students and their teachers alike. This impact seems to be as much cultural and political as it is medical and professional, but it is not less desirable for that reason.

Many U.S. educators have visited the program in Yugoslavia and have expressed their enthusiasm and support for it, as well as their feeling that it should be continued.

The Harvard evaluation team shares the view that the programs have had a favorable impact on the U.S., and would express concern only that the lack of reciprocity might generate certain negative implications among Yugoslavs who participate in the program. With the high priority apparently given to these programs by the Yugoslavs, however, they stand out as one of the more valuable components of the Special Foreign Currency Program in Yugoslavia.

Conferences

Eleven conferences, workshops, symposia, and seminars in Yugoslavia were financed by the Special Foreign Currency Program. The eleven conference type projects were:

1. International Conference of Cancer Epidemiology
2. Conference on Patient Education in Hospitals
3. Research Seminar and Meeting on International Psychotropic Drug Evaluation
4. Workshop of International Reference Center Network for Information on Psychotropic Drugs
5. Conference to Plan National Child Care Research
6. Conference of International Committee on Microbiological Specifications for Foods
7. International Epidemiological Research Conference
8. Symposium on Young Child Nutrition Programs: Evaluation and Guidelines
9. Planning Conference and Sixth Scientific Meeting of the International Epidemiological Association
10. Joint Working Conference of the Five Commissions of the International Union of Nutritional Sciences
11. International Conference on Community Water Supply Research and Development

The total expenditure for conferences was some $761,884, an average of approximately $70,000 per conference and represented about 3 percent of the total budget of the Special Foreign Currency Program in Yugoslavia.

The cost data for these eleven conferences are outlined in Table 5-3.

Relatively low cost is very often given as a reason for holding conferences in Yugoslavia. The cost-per-participant data in Table 5-3 have to be interpreted with some care, of course, since subsidies for international travel, per diems, and travel in Yugoslavia can vary from conference to conference. It would appear, however, that the cost of a typical conference in Yugoslavia is not particularly low.

Another reason often given for the organization of meetings in Yugoslavia is

Table 5-3

Summary of Conference Costs, Total Costs, Costs Per Participant, and Costs Per Participant Per Day

	Budget	Days of Meeting	Number of Participants	Cost Per Participant	Cost Per Participant Per Day
1.	$ 89,833	6	80[a]	$1,122	$187
2.	27,510	3	70	393	131
3.	20,000	5	28	714	143
4.	25,257	6	27	935	156
5.	28,150	7	28	1,005	144
6.	61,026	15	71	1,743	116
7.	132,344	11	164	807	73
8.	52,335	4	50[a]	1,047	262
9.	224,346	10	286	784	78
10.	47,083	4	57	826	206
11.	54,000	7	45	1,200	171
Totals	$761,884		906	$ 840	$103

[a]Projected number.

the "facility for travel of participants from widely different geographic and political areas of the world." For nine of the eleven conferences, data on the origin of the 587 participants are available. Participants come from many countries and included:

142 U.S.
131 Yugoslavia
 33 Communist countries (other than Yugoslavia)
210 Other industrial countries (as defined by the World Bank Yearbook)
 71 Other less-developed countries (as defined by the World Bank Yearbook)

Although the participation of Communist and less-developed countries did not approach that of the United States and Yugoslavia, it is necessary to realize that cultural, traditional, financial, and other factors serve to limit this participation. The overall mix in these meetings and the resulting contacts between scientists who otherwise would have little opportunity for knowing each other is very favorable, and should be further promoted. It would appear that the overall U.S. objective to increase international understanding is certainly served by these conferences. How much the Yugoslav health establishment benefits from them should be judged primarily by the Yugoslav evaluation team.

While most of the Harvard reviewers anticipated only a small or no impact on

U.S. domestic health objectives, naturally varying with the subject of the conference, a few expected some or a great potential impact. Almost all rated the actual or potential impact of the eleven conferences on the U.S. and Yugoslav scientific establishments, health care systems, and health manpower development as small or nonexistent.

In a sense, this generally unfavorable reaction by the Harvard reviewers may be misleading. It should be noted, for example, that all Harvard reviewers rated the proposed project objectives and the actual project accomplishments of the conferences in relation to the budget allocated at least as "some benefit." In fact, most responses to these two questions indicated significant potential benefit. Further, a number of uncoded comments tend to support a more favorable conclusion. Several of the reviewers' comments stress the "good organization," the "building of effective bridges between Yugoslav and Western scientists," the "encouragement to Yugoslav scientists to look westward," the "development of fairly objective means to evaluate the impact of psychotropic drugs in an international perspective," "the clear benefit to general East-West relations." On the other hand, a number of negative comments support a less favorable conclusion. The reviewers commented, for example, on "the question whether the vague, intangible but yet finite benefits [of the 6th Scientific Meeting of the International Epidemiological Association] justify the rather extreme cost"; on "the only good reason for these conferences in Yugoslavia [being] the availability of P.L. 480 money, which could be better used for other scientific purposes"; and on the fact that "conferences could have been held anywhere in the world."

The consensus seems to be that the conferences were very well organized, Yugoslav hospitality and effectiveness extraordinary, the international cultural and political impact very desirable; and that they were both enjoyable and professionally worthwhile for the participants. There is some question of how high a priority should be given to them in relation to scientific research, health care delivery, and health manpower projects. Perhaps the subjects dealt with in these conferences should be of greater relevance to Yugoslavia and they should have a greater voice in the planning and organization of these conferences.

Translations

One project involved the translation into English and subsequent printing in English of three Yugoslav biomedical journals. This project, with a total budget to date of some $742,378, was started in 1960 and terminated in 1972. It is one of the few projects that offer an opportunity to evaluate actual impact occurring over a period of years. The cover-to-cover translations of the *Archives of Biological Sciences, Acta Medica Jugoslavica*, and *Medical Journal* were done for more than ten years. The format of this project, which was really more a contract, closely followed the P.L. 480-financed contracts of the National Science Foundation for the translation of highly specialized foreign journals, books, and individual articles. This National Library of Medicine contract with the Nolit Publishing House in Belgrade provided for cover-to-cover translations of these journals. The obvious intent was to make available to the scientific communities of the United States and other English-speaking countries the best data published by the Yugoslav biomedical professions. This seemed particularly important, because U.S. scientists do tend to ignore literature published outside of the U.S., and are particularly reluctant to seek translations from languages they do not know. Therefore, the basic idea and goal of providing easier accessibility to foreign literature is very sound. For this project, it is possible to ascertain the extent to which this goal was reached.

A first relevant question is whether or not these three journals contained those articles which were of greatest interest to the English-speaking international scientific community. The Harvard evaluation team made three relatively straightforward investigations. First, during the visit to Yugoslavia, twenty-seven Yugoslav biomedical investigators, clinicians, and health officials were asked if they would choose these three journals as the most important and most worthy of cover-to-cover translation into English. The essence of their responses can be summarized as follows.

Journal	Should Be Included	Perhaps Should Be Included	Should Not Be Included	Unfamiliar with Journal
Archives of Biological Sciences	3	4	9	11
Acta Medica Jugoslavica	14	2	10	1
Medical Journal	9	8	10	—

Several Yugoslavs expressed the opinion that this contract should have been executed on their side by the academic and scientific societies rather than by the publishing company. In general, there was little enthusiasm for this project among the Yugoslavs, and only four out of the twenty-seven felt that it was a good method to "make Yugoslav scientific achievements better known throughout the world."

Second, an attempt was made to ascertain the extent to which these three translated journals were known by American scientists. Twenty-one biologists, 16 internists, 11 surgeons, 10 pediatricians, 9 obstetrician-gynecologists, and 12 public health specialists in academic departments were given the names of the three translated journals (identified as cover-to-cover translations of Yugoslav journals), and were asked if they had ever heard of the translated journal, and if they had ever used it. Their responses can be summarized as follows:

Scientists	#	Archives of Biological Sciences		Acta Medica Jugoslavica		Medical Journal	
		Heard of It	Used It	Heard of It	Used It	Heard of It	Used It
Biologists	21	5	2	3	0	3	0
Internists	16	0	0	4	2	3	2
Surgeons	11	0	0	3	2	3	0
Pediatricians	10	1	1	4	3	5	3
Obstetricians	9	0	0	3	2	2	2
Public health specialists	12	2	1	0	0	0	0

Clearly, very few American medical scientists have been directly aware of these journals. When the few who had used one or several of them were asked if they would have had specific articles translated, all answered in the affirmative; they would read and use these translated journals only to read specific articles, which they had found in the (rare) review sections of other journals or in one of the "Excerpts and Abstracts." Hence, it would appear that what impact the translated journals had had would not have been lost in the absence of the project. On balance, it does not seem that the translations added much to the use and availability of Yugoslav publications in the international scientific community.

Finally, a list was formed of twenty articles from each of the three journals, randomly chosen from three or four numbers in the fall of 1971 or spring of 1972. The list was given to 5 biologists, 5 internists, 4 surgeons, 3 pediatricians, 5 obstetrician-gynecologists, and 7 public health specialists, who were then asked how many of these articles they would read if they found them in a journal they were perusing. Their responses can be summarized as follows:

Of the 20 Articles Published in							
		Archives of Biological Sciences		Acta Medica Jugoslavica		Medical Journal	
		Scientists Would Read					
Scientists	#	Total	Average	Total	Average	Total	Average
Biologists	5	21	4.2	7	1.4	8	1.6
Internists	5	12	2.4	32	6.4	25	5.0
Surgeons	4	2	0.5	12	3.0	14	3.5
Pediatricians	3	4	1.3	18	6.0	13	3.3
Obstetricians	5	2	0.4	9	1.8	7	1.4
Public health specialists	7	3	0.7	19	2.7	23	3.3
Totals	29	44	1.5	97	3.3	90	3.1

If this small and somewhat superficial survey is any indication of the actual interest, the high costs of translation would not appear to be justified, even if these translations were widely available to the scientific community.

In 1968, Jacob Grauman of the Franklin Institute Research Laboratories, Science Information Services, under contract #PH-43-68-1032, prepared a report for the Department of Health, Education, and Welfare, Public Health Service, National Library of Medicine, entitled: "Evaluation of Technical Quality and Determination of Availability of 13 Health Science Serial Publications." Three of these publications were the Yugoslav journals translated into English (the other ten were Polish). This evaluation was written in November 1968, covering the availability for at least seven years of the translated journals in the U.S. The author examined several parameters, which would indicate the value of these translations; all investigations were done in the Philadelphia area.

Availability of Journals in the Philadelphia Medical Libraries

All three journals were available in eleven of the eighteen investigated libraries. The *Archives of Biological Sciences* was available in one additional library, the *Acta Medica Jugoslavica* in two additional libraries, and the *Medical Journal* in three additional libraries. Hence, in terms of general availability, the situation was certainly satisfactory.

Timeliness of Receipt of Journals

The Original-language Versions. The *Archives of Biological Sciences* is very irregularly published and the issues often arrived more than one year after the nominal date of publication in the College of Physicians Library in Philadelphia. The *Acta Medical Jugoslavica* arrived eight to ten months after the nominal date of publication, and the *Medical Journal* two to four months later than the nominal date of publication.

The English Language Versions. For the *Acta Medica Jugoslavica*, the lag between the nominal date of publication of the original language version and the publication in English was fourteen to eighteen months; for the *Medical Journal*, four to ten months; for the irregularly appearing *Archives of Biological Sciences*, it could not be ascertained. This long delay certainly impairs the value in terms of the originality and freshness of the articles.

Utilization of Copies of the Journals

None of the bound volumes of the three journals had even been borrowed in any of the Philadelphia libraries.

Utilization of the Journals by
Secondary Abstracting Services

Not one article of the three journals was abstracted in the *JAMA* between 1963 and 1967.

In the *Biological Abstracts*, 11 out of a sample of 40 articles published in the *Archives of Biological Sciences* and 6 out of a sample of 40 articles published in the *Acta Medica Jugoslavica* appeared as abstracts in 1963, and none in 1964. Out of a sample of 40 articles from the *Medical Journal*, no abstracts were published in 1963 and 1964.

Out of the same sample of 40 articles from each of the three journals in 1963 and 1964 (a total of 1040 articles), only three were abstracted in *Excerpta Medica* and two in *Chemical Abstracts*. (It is interesting to note that many more articles—at least ten times as many—from the ten Polish journals were abstracted.)

Obviously, the abstracting of these translations was low enough to be termed as almost insignificant.

As far as "editorial format, style, technical accuracy and completeness of English version of the three journals" are concerned, the Franklin Institute report rates them "quite good" (Archives of Biological Sciences), "high quality" (Acta Medica Jugoslavica), and "very high quality" (Medical Journal).

The summary of findings of this report is much more favorable concerning the value of these translations than the data warrant, an opinion shared by some of the interviewed scientists at the National Library of Medicine. Further, given that the ten Polish journal translations fared significantly better in the various evaluations than the three Yugoslav journals, the wisdom of the large expenditure for this project is subject to serious question.

The officials of the National Library of Medicine seem to share this point of view. They decided to stop this project, and the cover-to-cover translation of the three Yugoslav journals ceased in 1972. This decision to stop funding appears rather unusual for projects in the Special Foreign Currency Program, but one might wonder why it took so long for the decision to be reached.

If one wanted to utilize the obvious facility that the Yugoslavs have for languages and possibly also the relatively low cost of printing in Yugoslavia, one could propose a more critical selection of articles, of a real, timely, and more immediate interest, to the English readers, coming from a variety of Yugoslav sources and possibly other Eastern European sources. These articles, rapidly translated, printed, and more widely advertised and distributed, could make a much more relevant contribution than the discussed cover-to-cover translations which contain many articles of low interest, which are slowly published, are little known in the scientific community, and therefore used very little.

The question of whether or not these translation programs are of any value to Yugoslavia should be made by the Yugoslav scientists, who did not show much enthusiasm for them.

Critical Reviews

The National Library of Medicine contracted for four "Critical Reviews." Under these agreements, a Yugoslav principal investigator, usually with a team of collaborators, is supposed to review the world literature on a specific subject in depth and to prepare a comprehensive review in English. In a limited way, the National Library of Medicine provides assistance by "providing photocopies of needed articles not available to the principal investigator in his medical library" and by instituting "a reasonable number of demand searches of the MEDLARS system for bibliographic information starting in 1964."

The four subjects to be reviewed (with the total budgeted cost in parentheses) are:

1. Arachnidism, preparation of critical review ($16,022)

2. Primary Herpetic Infection, preparation of critical review ($ 6,802)

3. Critical review of "Epidemiology of Functional Psychoses" ($26,757)

4. Epidemiology of Gastric Cancer, preparation of critical review ($22,545)

The total amount budgeted for these projects accounts for only about 0.2 percent of the total budget of the Special Foreign Currency Program in Yugoslavia.

Several interviews with the U.S. project officers and a visit with two of the four Yugoslav principal investigators did not reveal any systematic planning for the choice of the subjects to be reviewed. They apparently were not chosen according to specific need for a particular subject to be reviewed or because of an unparalleled opportunity to obtain such a review in Yugoslavia. The choices seemed to be the result of somewhat haphazard encounters between Yugoslav scientists, interested and willing to do such a critical review of a subject in their specialty, and U.S. officials traveling in Yugoslavia.

The ability of many Yugoslav scientists to read several languages, their familiarity with the Eastern European literature, and their access to the literature retrieval systems in the U.S., certainly give them a special capability to "review the world literature." However, to do this in a broad field, like functional psychoses or epidemiology of gastric cancer, seemed to be an enormous task to the Harvard reviewers, and they uniformly saw only a "small advantage" of implementing this project in Yugoslavia rather than the U.S. For these two very broad, perhaps overambitious projects the reviewers also expected only a small or no contribution to the U.S. and Yugoslav scientific establishments, health care systems, and health manpower, and essentially no impact on U.S. domestic health objectives. They had to agree, however, that these two broad review projects, if they could be satisfactorily completed, would result in "great benefit" in relation to the amount of money allocated for their attainment.

The implementation in Yugoslavia of the two smaller review projects on arachnidism and primary herpetic infection was rated almost uniformly as being of "great advantage" in view of the special interest and competence of the principal investigators in Yugoslavia. As far as contribution to the Yugoslav and U.S. scientific establishments, health care systems, health manpower, and potential impact on U.S. domestic health objectives are concerned, however, these projects were rated slightly lower than the other two, presumably due to their limited breadth of application.

A final evaluation of these review projects naturally must await their completion, but even if they fulfill the broad objectives, it seems questionable if, without very careful planning and evidence of special interest and need, such literature review projects merit a very high priority rating. It might perhaps be advantageous to rely more on the Yugoslavs' familiarity with the Eastern European scientific establishment and literature, and to ask them to assist in making these more accessible, than to expect "world literature reviews."

The reviews of these four projects, as well as of the project "Translating into English and Printing in English 3 Yugoslav Biomedical Journals," indicate the need for a reappraisal of the planning for and the content of library-science oriented activities financed by the Special Foreign Currency Program in Yugoslavia and elsewhere.

6 Summary and Recommendations

Introduction

The Special Foreign Currency Program is an international health research program financed out of U.S.-owned foreign currency in excess of requirements as determined by the Treasury Department. The program has been in operation for thirteen years and presently is administered by the Office of International Health, and involves NIH, HSMHA, and FDA among the agencies of HEW. Over the years twelve countries have participated in the program.

Although the international health research program has grown in size and scope since its inception in fiscal 1961, the program is quite small in relation to the yearly operating budgets of the participating agencies. Nevertheless, the program can provide a valuable alternative resource for the achievement of domestic health objectives. Given the constraints upon the availability of dollars for the support of scientific activities, both in the United States and abroad, the utilization of excess foreign currencies is a valuable resource. Since a variety of important and unique research opportunities of potential usefulness exists in excess currency countries, the Special Foreign Currency Program is capable of developing knowledge and insights that might not otherwise be forthcoming.

In May 1971, the Department of Health, Education, and Welfare requested proposals to conduct an evaluative study of the impact of the Special Foreign Currency Program in Yugoslavia. The study was intended to evaluate the impact of the program on both the United States and Yugoslavia. The study was sponsored by the Division of Health Evaluation of the Department of Health, Education, and Welfare.

In general terms, according to the original request for proposals, the study was intended to assess the impact of the Special Foreign Currency Program in both countries, in order to bring about an improved program in the future. The study was designed to involve two separate, though integrated, evaluation projects, and two contracts were awarded. The assessment of the impact of the program on the United States was primarily the responsibility of an evaluation team at Harvard. The assessment of the impact of the program on Yugoslavia was primarily the responsibility of an evaluation team in Yugoslavia.

The two teams did coordinate their activities to mutual advantage. The basic strategies of evaluation and criteria for evaluation employed by the two teams were similar. A number of joint meetings were held involving several members of each team. Most important, the efforts of the two teams were mutually reenforcing. Since they were performing under separate contracts, each team was to submit a final report. The purpose of this report was to outline in appropriate detail the principal results of the evaluative efforts of the Harvard team.

As this study progressed, the participants came to appreciate that any evaluation, if it is to have its maximum potential effectiveness, must serve the needs of the decision-maker.

The parallel studies of impact in the two countries were specific to the Special Foreign Currency Program in Yugoslavia. The results of this evaluation effort will undoubtedly serve best the purpose of improving decisions in that program. The value of the study is not limited to this context, however. Obviously there should be much in this report that has potential value to decision-makers in other Special Foreign Currency Programs, in other health research programs, other research programs, and in general program management.

Principal Findings

It was apparently thought that the age of the program would make possible an actual impact orientation of the evaluation. The first thing that the Harvard evaluation team learned, however, was that the Special Foreign Currency Program in Yugoslavia in fact is overwhelmingly a recent program. Of the 110 projects evaluated, 51 had not started by the first of 1971. More significant, 95 of the projects were not scheduled to be completed by the end of 1971. Only nine projects began during the first six years of the program. Of the 15 projects scheduled to end by 1971, most were so recent that they had not yet attained publication, while other publications probably had not had the time to achieve near full impact. Thus, the evaluation had largely to involve projections of potential impact rather than attempts to measure actual impact.

Given that the program is so recent in terms of relative magnitudes, the implications for this evaluation study are somewhat mixed. On the one hand, it could be argued that the evaluation study was perhaps premature. Certainly in terms of assessing actual impact it must be judged premature. On the other hand, since evaluation should be designed to marshal information that will serve the purpose of improving decisions, the fact that a major proportion of program activity presumably is subject to future decisions augurs well for an earlier evaluation.

The major analytical efforts of the evaluation team were outlined in detail in Chapters 3, 4, and 5. Chapter 3 involved essentially an analysis of the trends in size and scope of the program and included data on the number of projects, the kinds of activities funded, and the levels of financial support. It was determined that the program had a rather slow start and that there was a rather dramatic increase in the size and scope of the program from 1967 on. In fact, of the 108 projects funded over the period 1960 through 1971, 12 were funded during the first seven years and 96 were funded during the next five years.

The analysis of the financial data led to the conclusion that HSMHA alone appears to have contributed to the rapid growth of the Special Foreign Currency Program in Yugoslavia from 1967 to 1969. It was over this three-year period that HSMHA assumed its dominant role in the overall program. Through 1966 HSMHA had funded eight projects at an original budget level of some $991,343 and NIH had funded four projects at an original budget level of some $910,878. But from 1967 through 1969 HSMHA funded 32 new projects at an original budget level of some $6.5 million, while NIH was funding only 5 new projects at an original budget level of only $238,589. In fact, by 1972 HSMHA had funded 70 projects, NIH had funded 32 projects, FDA had funded 7 projects, and EPA had funded a single project. Of the $25 million budgeted to date, HSMHA projects account for 75.4 percent, NIH projects for 19.3 percent, FDA projects for 5.1 percent, and the single EPA project for but 0.2 percent.

The financial data indicated other agency differences. NIH projects tend to involve the least amount of money, for example. The median budget for NIH projects is some $69,664, which is significantly less than the median budgets of HSMHA and FDA projects, $212,383 and $203,433 respectively. The median project lengths are also different: NIH and FDA projects have a median length of three years, while HSMHA projects have a median length of five years.

In part, these differences are consistent with differences in the kinds of activities funded. Laboratory research, clinical research, epidemiological research, and combinations of two or more of these are the major activity of the majority of the projects. Laboratory research tends to be dominated by NIH. Clinical research and epidemiological research tend to be the dominant activities of the HSMHA program. The much smaller FDA program appears to be roughly balanced among laboratory, clinical, and epidemiological research. These characteristics of the Special Foreign Currency Program in Yugoslavia seem consistent with the nature and objectives of the three agencies.

By far the most money is spent for epidemiological research. Some $10.8 million of the total budget to date of the program has been devoted to epidemiological research. Clinical and epidemiological research at $2.9 million; laboratory research at $1.8 million; laboratory and epidemiological research at $1.6 million; and clinical research at $1.2 million follow in order. These five types of research activities have accounted for almost 75 percent of the program's total budget to date.

HSMHA has spent much more on its program than the other agencies. This is due in part to the absolute size of the HSMHA program in terms of the number of projects supported, but it is also due to the fact that it tends to support longer projects and projects with larger budgets per year.

The objective of this study was to assess the impact of the Special Foreign Currency Program on both the United States and Yugoslavia. The primary technique for gathering data relevant to the impact of the projects involved a standard questionnaire for project review answered by the members of the two evaluation teams. The questionnaire was designed to provide information concerning relative progress, cooperative efforts, project impact, and other relevant information.

Given the recent nature of the program, the reviewers were assessing potential in the majority of cases. Further, of course, no universally accepted standards exist for measuring the effects upon a health care system or for gauging the results of health related research. An attempt has been made to obtain standards by asking a large group of competent consultants to read carefully through a large number of research projects and to answer a long series of difficult, judgmental questions. The answers to these questions were couched in what might be best described as "semiquantitative terms." Thus, they were asked if a particular project had the potential for making a maximal, a great, some, a small, or no contribution for example. Obviously, there is a significant subjective latitude in the understanding of these terms; equally obviously the result was not an objective measurement, but rather a subjective assessment. The strength of the assessment derives in part from the experience of the reviewers, but in the main from the averaging of multiple opinions. Finally, the main conclusions that were drawn from the responses were summative.

The reviewers' responses were outlined and analyzed in detail in Chapter 4. The principal conclusions drawn from the responses were:

1. In terms of whether or not the specific projects could be implemented in Yugoslavia to some advantage over implementing them in the United States, the Special Foreign Currency Program appears to do well. On average, the reviewers rated the projects between some advantage and great advantage for specific implementation in Yugoslavia.

2. A number of factors were identified that raised serious questions about the relative progress of certain projects. The program is characterized by amendments and cost overruns. In some instances the amendments and the increased costs were quite justified, but in a significant number of cases there is a clear indication that projects continued to get funding that perhaps should have been terminated.

3. The projects do tend to deal with important problems, but not with those of highest priority in either country. On balance, the reviewers rated the diseases, disorders, or conditions studied slightly more than important for the United States and somewhat more important for Yugoslavia. This would seem to be an appropriate set of circumstances—that is, this is not the only health research program in either country.

4. Although the number of responses was limited, the reviewers did rate the projects of the program as slightly better than comparable research projects known to them. Since it seems reasonable to speculate that the different

reviewers were more likely to be familiar with comparable projects in their own country, the Yugoslav response may indicate that the program involves some of that country's better researchers.

5. The reviewers were asked to rank the nonfinancial contributions of the U.S. in the form of such contributions as manpower, scientific guidance, and methodological support. The Yugoslav reviewers ranked this support as more than some, the Harvard reviewers between small and some. The importance of the nonfinancial support, particularly in terms of the role of the project officer, cannot be emphasized enough. The project officer can often make the difference between whether or not a project progresses in reasonable fashion. More significant, perhaps, the project officer can often directly affect the potential impact of a project by enhancing the dissemination of the results through publication in an appropriate English source.

6. A number of questions were included to gauge the general impact of the projects reviewed. In each case the Harvard reviewers assessed the impact to be somewhat lower than did the Yugoslav reviewers. In general, the impact on the scientific establishment was considered to be somewhat greater than the impact on the health care system for each country. The impact was considered to be somewhat less in the United States than it was in Yugoslavia.

Again in the context of general impact, the reviewers assessed the contributions to knowledge and to the stimulation of further research as more than small for the program as a whole.

7. The Harvard reviewers were asked to assess the potential impact of the program on the U.S. domestic health objectives. The program has more potential for impact on the objectives such as improved health information, preventive health care advances, morbidity reduction, and curing diseases. The program has less potential for impact on the objectives of improved geriatric care, improved treatment of mental disorders, and equitable and efficient costing arrangements. In the assessment of the single Harvard reviewer who had reviewed all projects, 81 percent of the projects are expected to make at least a small contribution to the U.S. domestic health objectives, 56 percent are expected to make at least some contribution, and 9 percent are expected to make a significant contribution. The assessment of the other Harvard reviewers was somewhat more favorable.

Certainly the relevant assessment of impact is appropriately the potential contribution per dollar expended. In these terms, the programs of NIH and FDA do somewhat better; the program of HSMHA does less well. The relative position of HSMHA would be somewhat less unfavorable if an adjustment were made for the propensity of HSMHA projects to make multiple contributions.

8. The Yugoslav reviewers were asked to assess the potential impact of the program on the Yugoslav domestic health objectives. Their responses reflect significantly more optimism for their country than those of the Harvard reviewers for the United States. The Yugoslavs rated 70 projects to have

potential for a significant contribution to at least one health objective and 105 of the 110 to have potential for some contribution to at least one health objective.

9. There is often a lag between the time research is completed and the results appear in the relevant literature. Further, there is usually some lag between the publication of research results and the general adoption of their implications. The Harvard reviewers were asked how long it would be before the results of a project would effect improvements in domestic health practice at a significant level if the results were published in either an American scientific or professional journal or in an official project report by HEW. The most striking thing about their responses was the similarity in the potential of private and government publication. Their responses indicate that HEW publication of research results is often a comparable alternative to publication in scientific and professional journals.

The questionnaires provided a large body of data. In all there were 56 responses for each of three reviewers for each of 110 projects. In order to gain additional insights a correlation analysis of the responses was undertaken, and was outlined in detail in Chapter 4. This analysis uncovered several important interactions among the variables that are relevant to the potential impact of the program. The principal inferences drawn from the correlation analysis were:

1. In essence, if projects are supported that deal with diseases, disorders, or conditions that are priority ones in Yugoslavia the project can be implemented to more advantage in Yugoslavia. Further, these projects are more likely to attract the better Yugoslav researchers. These factors may explain the higher potential these projects have for impact on the U.S. health care system.

2. Nonfinancial contributions are significantly correlated with actual project accomplishments. Further, when scientific guidance or methodological support is given to a specific project it has somewhat broader, more general implications.

3. There is a clear indication that laboratory research contributes more to the scientific establishment, while epidemiological research contributes more to the health care system.

4. Contributions to the scientific establishment and to the health care system tend to be correlated positively or negatively with specific health objectives, in a rather systematic pattern. Generally significant positive correlations obtain between the contribution to the scientific establishment and such health objectives as curing diseases, morbidity reduction, improved geriatric care, treatment of mental disorders, and improved health information; significant negative correlations obtain with the health objectives of promoting efficient health services delivery and equitable and efficient costing arrangements. On the other hand, generally significant positive correlations were observed between the contribution to the health care system and the health objectives of preventive

health care advances, promotion of a positive health life, efficient health services delivery, and solutions to environmental problems. Negative correlations were observed between the contributions to the health care system and the objectives of curing diseases, and improved treatment of mental disorders.

5. Systematic relationships among the ten U.S. domestic health objectives can be inferred from the correlation analysis. A reasonable relationship is implied by the correlations among curing diseases, morbidity reduction, and improved geriatric care. Obviously, morbidity reduction is generally associated with curing diseases, and the correlations imply that the potential contribution of the program to improved geriatric care is from curing diseases and affecting morbidity among the aged. The responses included many more projects making a contribution to curing diseases and morbidity reduction than to improved geriatric care, but the significant correlation indicates that those that are rated with a significant contribution to the latter also are rated with a significant contribution to both the former health objectives.

The correlations also imply a reasonable relationship among preventive health care advances, solutions to environmental problems, and promotion of a positive health life. Presumably, many projects that contribute to preventive health care advances and solutions to environmental problems involve consumer education, nutritional improvements, and the like. Further, preventive health care measures and those which promote the positive health life, such as consumer education and nutritional improvements, apparently represent reasonable ways to cope with certain of the problems associated with trends in industrialization, urbanization, population growth, and environmental impairment.

There are no other systematic relationships among the U.S. domestic health objectives implicit in the correlations among the reviewers' responses. Contributions to improved treatment of mental disorders, efficient health services delivery, equitable and efficient costing arrangements, and improved health information are not correlated with contributions to other objectives.

6. The correlation analysis implies that three factors tend to dominate the ratings of the contributions to U.S. domestic health objectives by the reviewers, the relative importance of the problem studied, the potential impact the results will have on the health care system, and the potential impact the results will have on the scientific establishment. The objectives of curing diseases, morbidity reduction, and improved treatment of mental disorders are associated only with the impact on the scientific establishment. The objective of efficient health services delivery is associated only with the impact on the health care system. The objectives of preventive health care advances, promotion of a positive health life, and solutions to environmental problems are associated with both relative importance and the impact on the health care system. The objective of improved health information is associated with both relative importance and impact on the scientific establishment. The objective of improved geriatric care is associated

with all three factors. Finally, the objective of equitable and efficient costing arrangements is not associated with any of the three factors.

7. The relative importance of the problem studied is significantly correlated with the time to effect impact for publication in either scientific or professional journals or HEW project reports. The correlation analysis does imply that contributions to certain U.S. domestic health objectives are likely to effect improvements in a shorter length of time from publication in HEW reports, or, alternatively, that such results are more likely to be published in HEW reports. Potential contributions to the objectives of morbidity reduction, promotion of positive health life, and solutions to environmental problems are more significantly correlated with the time to effect impact if published only in HEW reports than with the time to effect impact if published in scientific or professional journals.

Further analysis in Chapter 4 led to certain other conclusions:

1. The reviewers expressed serious doubts as to whether fifteen of the projects ever had any potential for making contributions to U.S. domestic health objectives.

2. Several projects can be criticized for the data-processing techniques of the research team.

3. The research promised by some proposals did not merit funding with Special Foreign Currency Program monies. In this context, the objections raised by scientific reviewers were too often ignored and the proposals approved without change.

4. Many problems have arisen because the project approval process is often exceedingly slow.

5. Many problems have arisen because the monitoring role of project officers is often less than appropriate.

6. The potential impact of the program would be considerably enhanced if more attention were paid to seeking appropriate American publication of research results.

Chapter 5 was devoted to certain in-depth analyses. First, the impact of nine completed projects was assessed. On balance, it would appear that most of the nine completed projects have begun to have impact on the United States. In seven of the nine cases, more specialists in the field of the study interviewed knew of the project than did not. This is perhaps encouraging, considering that in many cases there were not a significant number of publications. Further, in eight of the nine cases the specialists appear to have rather high opinions of the projects.

Still, almost half of the specialists contacted either did not know of the project or were only vaguely aware of it, even though the subject matter was in their special field of interest. The stimulation of and assistance in writing more well-read publications still seems to be a neglected aspect of the U.S. collaboration, and should be emphasized as an obligation of the project officers.

Second, since approximately a quarter of the projects of the program involve somewhat unique activities an attempt was made to assess their potential impact separately. In brief:

1. The student exchange program on balance has had a favorable impact on the United States. The major defect in the program that was uncovered by a complete survey of the participants involved the lack of any systematic briefing of the students before they embarked for Yugoslavia.

2. Ten percent of all projects were conferences. The reasons most often cited for supporting conferences in Yugoslavia are that they are relatively inexpensive, and that Yugoslavia facilitates participation from widely different geographic and political areas of the world. The analysis of these conferences lends some support to the latter reason, but not to the former. The consensus seems to be that the conferences were well organized, the Yugoslav hospitality and effectiveness extraordinary, and the international cultural and political impact desirable, and that they were both enjoyable and professionally worthwhile for the participants. There is some question of how high a priority should be given to conferences in relation to scientific research and health care delivery research.

3. One project involved the translation into English and subsequent printing in English of three Yugoslav biomedical journals. This project had a total budget of some $742,378 and was in operation from 1960 through 1972. By virtually any criterion, this project is rated unfavorably.

4. Four projects were funded to provide critical reviews of world literature on specific subjects. A final evaluation of these review projects must await their completion, but even if they fulfill the broad objectives, whether such projects merit a very high priority rating is subject to serious question.

Recommendations

The value of this study in the last analysis will be determined by the extent to which the information provided is useful to the relevant decision-maker. In this sense, the primary recommendation has to be that the relevant decision-makers read the report carefully and extract that information which contributes to their decision-making process. Still, implicit in the principal findings are a number of specific recommendations.

The general nature of the Special Foreign Currency Program is such that the role of the project officer is of signal importance to the potential impact of the program. In the context of the appointment of project officers three recommendations seem to be in order. First, care should be taken to appoint as project officers only individuals who by their scientific training and research experience can understand all aspects of the research project, and give substantial assistance at all stages, particularly in the preparation of the research protocol, in budgeting, in preparing requests for amendments, and in the publication of research papers in appropriate journals. Second, if for any reason a project officer is appointed who does not have the prescribed training and experience, a consultant should be appointed who will give professional assistance as required. Third, the role of the project officer should be more fully described in the agreement, and the tasks he should perform at each stage of the project should be specified.

Three recommendations are also in order concerning project monitoring. First, the project officer should be required to report at least once a year on the progress of the project. Such reports should complement, not replace, the trip reports made after each visit to the project and should summarize developments of the project and record all decisions made by the project officer. Second, the opinions of the project officer should be recorded on each item of any proposed amendment to the agreement. The views of any consultant and of the original review team should also be obtained and kept in the record. Third, all correspondence between the principal investigator and the project officer should be included in the master file of each project to provide background for all decisions made by the project officer relating to the project.

It is strongly recommended that a policy be established requiring that trip reports should uniformly deal with every aspect of the project, including progress to date, problems that have arisen, status of supplies and equipment, results achieved, and proposals, if any, for amendments of the original agreement.

It is most strongly recommended that the project officer should be made responsible for ensuring appropriate publication of reports of the research done in each project.

The role of the project officer is sufficiently important to the potential impact of the program that such recommendations as would affect this role to some advantage are appropriately emphasized. But certain other specific recommendations seem appropriate.

It is recommended that serious consideration be given to providing for more rapid review for all project applications.

Many projects have data-processing difficulties. Program personnel in the agencies seem generally aware of the kinds of problems associated with data handling. It is recommended that agency program heads and review sections, however, give particular attention to the data-processing question, and institute a mechanism to identify the occasional project that has not foreseen or prepared for its data-processing needs.

It is recommended that a systematic check be instituted to assess the extent to which the constructive suggestions made by study sections are acted upon.

It is recommended that OIH examine cases in which the requirement that projects be beneficial to both countries is not met, and impede the funding of new projects that ignore the health needs of the United States.

Finally, it is recommended that OIH make appropriate changes in the process by which the relative shares of the several agencies are determined in order to remove the incentive for each agency to continue to support existing projects which should be terminated.

Postscript

Postscript: The Final Report of the Yugoslav Team

After the completion of the report by the Harvard University team the final report of the Yugoslav evaluation team became available. It seems appropriate at this point to summarize the major findings and conclusions presented by the Yugoslav team in their report.

The members of the Yugoslav team were:

Dr. Ljubomir Božović, Chairman
Professor, Faculty of Medicine
University of Zagreb

Dr. Milutin Nešković
Professor Emeritus, Faculty of Medicine
University of Beograd

Dr. Ernest Grin
Professor, Faculty of Medicine
University of Sarajevo

Dr. Miroslav Radovanović
Professor, Faculty of Medicine
University of Novi Sad

Dr. Sead Huković
Professor, Faculty of Medicine
University of Sarajevo

Dr. Franc Erjavec
Professor, Faculty of Medicine
University of Ljubljana

Dr. Berislav Skupnjak, Under Secretary
Secretariat for Health and Social Welfare of SR of Croatia
Zagreb

Dr. Božidar Čolaković
Docent, Faculty of Medicine
University of Beograd
Director of the Institute of Public Health of SR of Serbia
Beograd

Dr. Nikola Serafimov
Docent, Faculty of Medicine
University of Skopje

Dr. Nikola Kovačević
Institute of Marine Biology
Kotor

In general the Yugoslav team used the same evaluative instruments, and their report resembles the one produced by the Harvard team. Certain points should be emphasized, however, that derive both from the different vantage views of the teams and from the Yugoslavs' assessment of the nature of Yugoslavia as a country and the impact that the research projects had on it. For example, more confidence can be placed in the Yugoslav evaluation of the impact of the program on Yugoslavia than the American evaluation of such an impact, since the Yugoslav team was in a better position to evaluate the needs of its own country and to assess the nature and quality of research efforts of Yugoslav scientists. Thus certain characteristics of the Yugoslav scene that have a bearing on the program can be singled out:

1. Yugoslavia is smaller, less developed, and economically poorer than the United States. A little goes a long way in Yugoslavia compared to the United States, and marginal increments in research funds will have a greater impact because of the relatively small size of the research establishment to begin with.

2. Manpower is more easily available in Yugoslavia and relatively less costly than in the United States. Thus research can be conducted less expensively than similar research in the U.S.

3. Certain types of research—epidemiological research, for example—can be carried out somewhat better in Yugoslavia than in the United States, because of greater control over population samples and a higher response rate.

4. The Yugoslav team rated the impact of the program in Yugoslavia consistently higher than the Harvard team did, presumably because it knew the situation better at home, and because existing levels were quite low.

5. A most important by-product of the research program, as seen from the Yugoslav side, was its impact on the reduction of the brain drain from Yugoslavia. Since the program helped to build a research capacity in Yugoslavia, the country can more easily keep its scientists instead of losing them to research institutions abroad.

It is also reassuring to note that in almost all instances, the evaluations and the conclusions concerning the various components of the Special Foreign Currency program under investigation were either identical or very similar to those of the Harvard team. Among these we can single out:

1. The advice that greater care should be exercised and pilot studies conducted before embarking on very large projects and committing considerable amounts of money for extended periods of time.

2. The strong support for basic research.

3. The positive attitude toward well-planned epidemiological investigations.

4. The considerable value attributed to the student exchange program.

5. The feeling that a more critical attitude should be adopted in the selection of, and preparation for, international conferences held in Yugoslavia.

6. The low evaluation given to the program of translation of journals and the writing of critical reviews.

Certain remarks made by the Yugoslav team about the selection process of the projects are also worthy of note:

1. There is a felt need to improve the selection process within Yugoslavia, and the Yugoslavs provided specific suggestions for such improvements.

2. The Yugoslavs also noted that the criteria of the different agencies (NIH, HSMHA, etc.) varied, and that in some instances one agency was affected by strictly scientific criteria, and another by areas of priority.

3. In some instances, the knowledge that the project would most likely be approved by the American side made the Yugoslav review less thorough.

4. The fact that twice as many of the projects were associated with nonuniversity institutions or only indirectly connected with universities as were associated with universities was negatively evaluated by the Yugoslav team. They felt that universities were better equipped to pass judgment on research projects. They also felt that in some instances researchers changed their field of research solely to get research funding; this would be less likely to happen if universities played a more important role in the selection process.

The "general conclusions" reached by the Yugoslav team were the following:

1. The collaboration between the United States and Yugoslavia in the 110 evaluated projects was, for the most part, very beneficial to Yugoslavia.

2. The benefit was primarily manifested in the introduction of new methods into Yugoslav scientific research; epidemiologic methods, for example.

3. Many Yugoslav scientists visited many interesting research institutions in different countries, and thus made good contacts and relations not only with American scientists but also with scientists from other countries. The institutional and personal contacts created will assuredly influence the scientific collaboration between the two countries long after the termination of the Special Foreign Currency Program.

4. The invested funds gave reasonably good results, which cannot be expressed in terms of money because they are primarily in the sphere of "social returns," and also "potential" in their promises.

5. One of the most positive results, already noted, was the prevention of the brain drain from Yugoslavia and the creation of a scientific atmosphere in the host country.

6. Some of the projects, which were not research oriented such as student exchanges, were also positively evaluated.

7. Translations of journals and the writing of critical reviews were examples of projects that should not be financed in the future.

8. Although the benefit of conferences was relatively high for the participants, in the future more care should be exercised in preparation for these conferences.

Recommendations

1. One independent review committee for all project proposals should be formed in Yugoslavia. "Independent" means that the members of the committee could not obtain funds from the Special Foreign Currency Program. This committee should have an advisory and coordinating function in relation to the counterpart committees in each Republic.

2. All information about a project proposal should be available to this committee, including letters from the potential project officer.

3. All progress reports and information from trip reports of project officers relevant to the progress of the project should also be available to the Yugoslav committee.

4. The possibility should exist that by agreement between the Yugoslav committee and a corresponding U.S. agency a project could be discontinued if its progress was not deemed satisfactory.

5. The role of the project officer should be better defined. One of the most important parts of this definition should be that a project officer be responsible only for one project.

6. It would be very useful if different U.S. agencies would in the future apply the same criteria in reviewing proposals.

7. For large and expensive projects, the method of pilot study should be used more than it has been to date, to avoid the spending of large sums on projects that will not give significant results.

8. It is absolutely necessary to support basic research, because of the indirect effect of this kind of research in creating the necessary flavor of quality and the training of compotent personnel for applied research.

9. In Yugoslavia the competition of different institutions for the same project should be stimulated.

10. In spite of the criticism expressed, epidemiological projects should be supported in the future, but they should be planned more carefully. The reason for such a recommendation is that there have been some excellent projects in the present program.

11. On the basis of the present study, it is strongly recommended that the collaborative efforts of both countries in solving common problems of research in health be maintained.

Appendix

An Evaluative Study of the Impact of the Special Activities Overseas Program: Questionnaire for Project Review

Name of reviewer

Project number

Project title

Introduction: This questionnaire has been designed to elicit important information in eight critical areas. In each area a number of questions are listed which should provide certain information. There are a total of 36 questions. Please answer all that are relevant for the particular project you have just completed reviewing basing your answers only upon the project file you have just reviewed.

All questions are designed such that your response can be recorded on a scale from 1 (high) to 5 (low) except where there are contrary instructions. In any case where the information necessary to answer the question is not available in the project file please answer 6 (not known). The category "not applicable" numbered 7 is also provided. In many cases you may feel that additional information can be supplied. Space has been furnished for comments. Please comment whenever you deem appropriate.

1—Maximal benefit . . . or . . . To a very marked degree . . . etc.
2—Great benefit . . . . . or . . . To a marked degree . . . . etc.
3—Some benefit . . . . . or . . . To a moderate degree . . . . . etc.
4—Small benefit . . . . . or . . . To a minor degree . . . . etc.
5—No benefit . . . . or . . . Not at all . . . . etc.
6—Not known . . . .
7—Not applicable . . . .

I. Administrative Information

1. For how many years was the original award to this project?

   years   From   To

2. What proportion of the time of the award had expired as of the latest information in the project file?

3. What was the total budget approved and funded from U.S. source (to the nearest thousand dollars)?

4. What was the financial contribution of Yugoslavia, if any?

153

II.   Relative Progress of the Project

5.   Has the project made reasonable progress in terms of the original time schedule?

Yes

No

6.   Have any significant cost overruns been incurred?

Yes

No   .

7.   Rate the proposed project objectives in relation to the amount of money allocated for their attainment.

1—Maximal benefit
2—Great benefit
3—Some benefit
4—Small benefit
5—No benefit
6—Not known
7—Not applicable

8.   Rate the actual project accomplishments in relation to the amount of money allocated for their attainment.

1—Maximal benefit
2—Great benefit
3—Some benefit
4—Small benefit
5—No benefit
6—Not known
7—Not applicable

9.   Rate the significance of the specific advantages—for example, special institutional capabilities of expertise, high disease incidence or unique disease aspects—of implementing this project in Yugoslavia rather than the U.S.

1—Maximal advantage
2—Great advantage
3—Some advantage
4—Small advantage
5—No advantage
6—Not known
7—Not applicable

III. General Information Relative to the Project

10. Rate the relative importance for Yugoslavia of the diseases, disorders, or conditions studied.

  1—Most important
  2—Very important
  3—Important
  4—Not very important
  5—Not important
  6—Not known
  7—Not applicable

11. Rate the relative importance for the U.S. of the diseases, disorders, or conditions studied.

  1—Most important
  2—Very important
  3—Important
  4—Not very important
  5—Not important
  6—Not known
  7—Not applicable

12. Classify the project by type or types:

  1. Laboratory research
  2. Clinical research
  3. Epidemiological research
  4. Conference
  5. Manpower training
  6. Student exchange
  7. Translation
  8. Critical review
  9. Construction
  10. Other

13. Rate the prevalence in the U.S. of the disease, disorder, or condition studied, that is, how many people now have it?

  1—Very high
  2—High
  3—Moderate
  4—Low
  5—Very low
  6—Not known
  7—Not applicable

14. Rate the incidence in the U.S., that is, how many new cases arise in this country each year?

       1—Very high
       2—High
       3—Moderate
       4—Low
       5—Very low
       6—Not known
       7—Not applicable

15. Identify comparable research projects carried out, if any are known to you, here or abroad.

       1.
       2.
       3.

16. How does this project compare with those named in question 15?

       1—Very much better
       2—Somewhat better
       3—About the same
       4—Not quite as good
       5—Much worse
       6—Not known
       7—Not applicable

IV. Cooperative Efforts—U.S. Contributions Other Than Financial Contributions

17. What was the extent of any U.S. contribution of manpower, scientific guidance, methodological support, and the like to this project?

       1—Maximal contribution
       2—Great contribution
       3—Some contribution
       4—Small contribution
       5—No contribution
       6—Not known
       7—Not applicable

18. What was the extent of any contribution to this project by parties other than the U.S. and Yugoslavia?

       1—Maximal contribution
       2—Great contribution
       3—Some contribution

4—Small contribution
5—No contribution
6—Not known
7—Not applicable

V. Project Impact—Actual for Completed Projects; Potential for Uncompleted Projects

19. Rate the contribution to the Yugoslav scientific establishment.

1—Maximal contribution
2—Great contribution
3—Some contribution
4—Small contribution
5—No contribution
6—Not known
7—Not applicable

20. Rate the contribution to the Yugoslav health care system.

1—Maximal contribution
2—Great contribution
3—Some contribution
4—Small contribution
5—No contribution
6—Not known
7—Not applicable

21. Rate the contribution to the U.S. scientific establishment.

1—Maximal contribution
2—Great contribution
3—Some contribution
4—Small contribution
5—No contribution
6—Not known
7—Not applicable

22. Rate the contribution to the U.S. health care system.

1—Maximal contribution
2—Great contribution
3—Some contribution
4—Small contribution
5—No contribution
6—Not known
7—Not applicable

23. Rate the contribution to the development of Yugoslav health manpower.

       1—Maximal contribution
       2—Great contribution
       3—Some contribution
       4—Small contribution
       5—No contribution
       6—Not known
       7—Not applicable

24. Rate the contribution to the development of U.S. health manpower.

       1—Maximal contribution
       2—Great contribution
       3—Some contribution
       4—Small contribution
       5—No contribution
       6—Not known
       7—Not applicable

25. Rate the impact, if any, of this project on any country or countries other than Yugoslavia or the U.S.

       1—Maximal impact
       2—Great impact
       3—Some impact
       4—Small impact
       5—No impact
       6—Not known
       7—Not applicable

26. Rate the contribution of this project in terms of stimulation of further research.

       1—Maximal contribution
       2—Great contribution
       3—Some contribution
       4—Small contribution
       5—No contribution
       6—Not known
       7—Not applicable

27. According to the project file how many publications have appeared or been accepted to appear in scientific or professional journals in:

    a. Yugoslav language   number

                                        reference

    b. English   number

                                    reference

    c. Other   language   number

                                    reference

28. Rate the contribution of this project to medical knowledge or other health related knowledge.

        1—Maximal contribution
        2—Great contribution
        3—Some contribution
        4—Small contribution
        5—No contribution
        6—Not known
        7—Not applicable

29. Have significant project benefits occurred that were not anticipated in the project protocol? Briefly specify.

    Yes

    No

VI. Impact on U.S. Domestic Health Objectives

30. For each of the ten domestic health objectives listed below rate the contribution of this project. Indicate in the space provided the diseases, disorders, or conditions whose amelioration this project seeks to affect. For example, a syphilitic treatment project might be rated for 1., 2., and 3. and the word "syphilis" indicated.

    1. Curing diseases and organic dysfunctions or impairments

            1—Maximal contribution
            2—Great contribution
            3—Some contribution
            4—Small contribution
            5—No contribution
            6—Not known
            7—Not applicable

    2. Morbidity reduction

            1—Maximal contribution
            2—Great contribution
            3—Some contribution
            4—Small contribution

5—No contribution
6—Not known
7—Not applicable

3. Preventive health care advances

    1—Maximal contribution
    2—Great contribution
    3—Some contribution
    4—Small contribution
    5—No contribution
    6—Not known
    7—Not applicable

4. Promotion of a positive health life (e.g., consumer education and nutritional improvements)

    1—Maximal contribution
    2—Great contribution
    3—Some contribution
    4—Small contribution
    5—No contribution
    6—Not known
    7—Not applicable

5. Improved geriatric care and degenerative disease reduction

    1—Maximal contribution
    2—Great contribution
    3—Some contribution
    4—Small contribution
    5—No contribution
    6—Not known
    7—Not applicable

6. Improved treatment for mental disorders

    1—Maximal contribution
    2—Great contribution
    3—Some contribution
    4—Small contribution
    5—No contribution
    6—Not known
    7—Not applicable

7. Efficient health services delivery: institutional improvements, more efficient manpower use, and increased manpower.

    1—Maximal contribution
    2—Great contribution

3—Some contribution
4—Small contribution
5—No contribution
6—Not known
7—Not applicable

8. Equitable and efficient costing arrangements

    1—Maximal contribution
    2—Great contribution
    3—Some contribution
    4—Small contribution
    5—No contribution
    6—Not known
    7—Not applicable

9. Solutions to the problems raised by the secular societal trends of industrialization, urbanization, population growth, and environmental impairment

    1—Maximal contribution
    2—Great contribution
    3—Some contribution
    4—Small contribution
    5—No contribution
    6—Not known
    7—Not applicable

10. Improved health information, health information exchange, and statistical methods

    1—Maximal contribution
    2—Great contribution
    3—Some contribution
    4—Small contribution
    5—No contribution
    6—Not known
    7—Not applicable

VII. Additional Information

31. Assuming that the results of this project are to be written up in an American scientific or professional journal, how long will it be until those results effect improvements in domestic health practice at a significant level?

    1—Immediately
    2—After a short length of time

3—After a moderate length of time
4—After a long length of time
5—Never
6—Not known
7—Not applicable

32. Assuming the only English language publication to be the DHEW official project report, how long will it be until those results effect improvements in domestic health practice at a significant level? (If other English publication has already occurred, do not answer.)

1—Immediately
2—After a short length of time
3—After a moderate length of time
4—After a long length of time
5—Never
6—Not known
7—Not applicable

VIII. Subjective Evaluation

33. Considering only the questions you have answered, how much confidence would you place upon those answers?

1—Extreme confidence
2—Reasonable confidence
3—Moderate confidence
4—Some confidence
5—Little confidence

34. Do you think an outside specialist should be consulted?

Name

Address

Phone number (if known)

35. Are there any specific tasks which you think the staff should complete in order to provide a more comprehensive review of this project?

36. Additional comments:

Table A-1

Variables Included in the Correlation Analysis

Variable Number	Variable	Response to Question Number
1	Reasonable progress	5
2	Cost overruns	6
3	Proposed objectives relative to budget allocated	7
4	Actual accomplishments relative to budget allocated	8
5	Specific advantages of implementing in Yugoslavia	9
6	Relative importance for Yugoslavia of disease, disorder, or condition studied	10
7	Relative importance for U.S. of disease, disorder, or condition studied	11
8	Prevalence of the disease, disorder, or condition studied	13
9	Incidence of the disease, disorder, or condition studied	14
10	Number of comparable research projects known to reviewer	15
11	Comparison of project with comparable research projects	16
12	U.S. nonfinancial contributions	17
13	Third-country contributions	18
14	Contribution to Yugoslav scientific establishment	19
15	Contribution to Yugoslav health care system	20
16	Contribution to U.S. scientific establishment	21
17	Contribution to U.S. health care system	22
18	Contribution to Yugoslav health manpower development	23
19	Contribution to U.S. health manpower development	24
20	Third-country impact	25
21	Contribution to stimulation of further research	26
22	Number of Serbo-Croatian publications	27
23	Number of English publications	27
24	Number of other language publications	27
25	Contribution to knowledge	28
26	Unanticipated project benefits	29
27	Contribution to objective curing diseases	30.1
28	Contribution to objective morbidity reduction	30.2
29	Contribution to objective preventive health care advances	30.3
30	Contribution to objective promote positive health life	30.4
31	Contribution to objective improved geriatric care	30.5
32	Contribution to objective improved treatment of mental disorders	30.6

Table A-1 (cont.)

Variable Number	Variable	Response to Question Number
33	Contribution to objective efficient health services delivery	30.7
34	Contribution to objective equitable and efficient costing arrangements	30.8
35	Contribution to objective solutions to environmental problems	30.9
36	Contribution to objective improved health information	30.10
37	Time to effect improvements if published in scientific or professional journal	31
38	Time to effect improvements if published in official HEW project report	32
39	Reviewer's confidence	33

Table A-2
Correlation Matrix of all Reviewers' Responses

CORRELATION COEFFICIENTS

VARIABLE DESCRIPTION	VAR(1)	VAR(2)	VAR(3)	VAR(4)	VAR(5)	VAK(6)	VAR(7)	VAR(10)	VAR(11)	VAR(12)
VAR(1)	1.000	-0.255**	0.082	0.169	-0.176	-0.028	-0.062	-0.001	-0.139	-0.038
VAR(2)	-0.255**	1.000	-0.014	0.083	0.277**	0.057	0.011	-0.089	0.089	0.280**
VAR(3)	0.082	-0.014	1.000	0.387***	0.325***	0.211**	0.180	0.046	0.319*	0.028
VAR(4)	0.169	0.083	0.387***	1.000	0.120	0.145	0.170	0.158	0.228	-0.322***
VAR(5)	-0.176	0.277**	0.325***	0.120	1.000	0.238*	0.170	-0.021	0.274**	-0.027
VAR(6)	-0.028	0.057	0.211**	0.145	0.238*	1.000	0.590***	0.057	0.213	0.222*
VAR(7)	-0.062	0.011	0.180	0.170	0.170	0.590***	1.000	0.334***	0.230	0.216*
VAR(10)	-0.001	-0.089	0.046	0.158	-0.021	0.057	0.334***	1.000	0.031	0.118
VAR(11)	-0.139	0.089	0.319*	0.228	0.274**	0.213	0.230	0.031	1.000	0.065
VAR(12)	-0.038	0.280**	0.028	-0.322***	-0.027	0.222*	0.216*	0.118	0.065	1.000
VAR(13)	-0.119	0.299*	0.097	0.244**	-0.034	0.102	0.201*	0.271*	0.282**	0.525***
VAR(14)	-0.057	-0.033	0.221*	0.226*	-0.123	-0.222*	-0.043	0.110	0.272*	0.212*
VAR(15)	-0.065	0.140	0.041	0.175	0.264**	-0.160	0.167	0.162	-0.101	0.268**
VAR(16)	-0.072	0.080	0.343***	0.181	0.107	-0.527***	0.339***	-0.012	0.212	0.214*
VAR(17)	-0.216*	0.192**	0.212*	0.151	0.414***	-0.026	0.295***	0.156	0.244	0.147
VAR(18)	0.068	0.173	0.166	0.242*	0.274**	0.291**	0.213*	0.128	0.118	0.361***
VAR(19)	0.114	-0.221*	0.028	0.176	0.277**	0.327***	-0.221*	0.120	-0.078	-0.056
VAR(20)	-0.123	-0.030	0.371***	0.049	0.112	0.167	0.049	0.013	0.234	-0.153
VAR(21)	-0.049	-0.032	0.263***	0.292**	-0.049	0.151	0.005	0.104	0.205	-0.255**
VAR(22)	0.098	-0.390*	-0.233	0.065	-0.143	-0.080	0.195	-0.034	-0.310	-0.164
VAR(23)	0.378*	-0.280	-0.228	-0.248	0.065	-0.181	-0.470	-0.194	-0.143	-0.225
VAR(24)	0.639	0.132	-0.712	-0.424	-0.352	-0.352	-0.074	-0.423	-0.649	-0.676
VAR(25)	-0.126	-0.103	0.306**	0.099	0.037	-0.252	0.018	0.022	0.341**	-0.084
VAR(26)	-0.002	0.180	0.143	0.164	0.085	-0.085	0.350***	0.031	0.194	-0.255**
VAR(37)	-0.075	-0.125	0.435***	-0.034	0.157	0.010	0.321***	-0.054	0.186	-0.109
VAR(38)	-0.055	-0.190*	0.331***	-0.043	0.076	0.333***	0.291***	0.013	-0.167	-0.035
VAR(39)	0.292**	-0.044	0.215*	0.218*	0.251**	0.395***	0.291***	0.115	-0.046	0.073

Table A-2 (cont.)

CORRELATION COEFFICIENTS

VARIABLE DESCRIPTION	VAR (13)	VAR (14)	VAR (15)	VAR (16)	VAR (17)	VAR (18)	VAR (19)	VAR (20)	VAR (21)	VAR (22)
VAR(1)	-0.057	-0.119	-0.065	-0.072	-0.216*	0.068	0.114	-0.123	-0.049	0.098
VAR(2)	0.239*	-0.033	0.140	0.080	0.192*	0.173	0.221*	-0.030	-0.032	-0.390*
VAR(3)	0.097	0.221*	0.041	0.343***	0.212*	0.166	0.028	0.371***	0.263**	-0.233
VAR(4)	-0.244*	-0.226*	0.175	0.181	0.151	0.242*	0.176	0.049	0.292***	0.065
VAR(5)	-0.034	-0.160	0.264**	0.107	0.291***	0.274***	0.167	0.112	-0.080	-0.143
VAR(6)	0.102	-0.043	0.527***	-0.026	0.339***	0.327***	0.213*	0.151	-0.049	-0.181
VAR(7)	0.201*	0.110	0.414***	0.167	0.156	0.295***	0.120	0.221*	0.049	0.005
VAR(10)	0.271*	0.272*	0.162	-0.012	0.244	0.128	0.078	0.013	0.104	0.034
VAR(11)	-0.282*	-0.212*	0.101	0.212	0.147	0.118	0.056	0.234	0.205	-0.310
VAR(12)	0.525***	0.077	0.268**	0.214*	0.172	0.361***	0.143	0.153	0.255**	-0.164
VAR(13)	1.000	0.077	0.201*	0.182	0.172	0.159	0.143	0.295**	0.233***	-0.172
VAR(14)	0.077	1.000	-0.182	0.622***	-0.081	0.235*	0.051	0.120	0.533***	-0.234
VAR(15)	0.201*	-0.182	1.000	-0.123	0.481***	0.468***	0.051	0.222*	0.068	0.027
VAR(16)	0.182	0.622***	-0.123	1.000	-0.027	0.163	0.040	0.232*	0.511***	-0.179
VAR(17)	0.172	-0.081	0.481***	-0.027	1.000	0.172	0.279***	0.293**	-0.077	-0.046
VAR(18)	0.159	0.235*	0.468***	0.163	0.172	1.000	0.405***	0.032	-0.240*	-0.193
VAR(19)	0.143	0.051	0.051	0.040	0.279***	0.405***	1.000	-0.198*	-0.190*	-0.302
VAR(20)	0.295**	0.120	0.222*	0.232*	0.293**	0.032	-0.198*	1.000	0.455***	0.058
VAR(21)	0.233***	0.533***	0.068	0.511***	-0.077	-0.240*	-0.190*	0.455***	1.000	0.119
VAR(22)	-0.172	-0.234	0.027	-0.179	-0.046	-0.193	-0.302	0.058	0.119	1.000
VAR(23)	-0.465**	-0.308	0.152	-0.117	-0.100	0.138	-0.280	0.049	-0.268	0.349
VAR(24)	-0.837	-0.802	0.755	-0.919	0.925	-0.380	-0.871	-0.941	-0.422	0.945
VAR(25)	-0.107	0.321***	-0.200*	0.208*	0.098	-0.095	0.175	0.365***	0.418***	-0.182
VAR(26)	0.239*	0.239*	-0.067	0.080	0.016	0.149	0.175	0.069	0.134	-0.541**
VAR(37)	-0.052	0.036	0.168	0.084	0.239*	0.271**	-0.045	0.282**	-0.103	-0.200
VAR(38)	-0.061	0.004	0.209*	-0.044	0.338***	0.115	-0.125	0.350***	0.195*	-0.116
VAR(39)	0.179	-0.230*	0.412***	-0.044	0.156	0.322***	0.241*	-0.092	-0.226*	0.185

Table A-2 (cont.)

CORRELATION COEFFICIENTS

VARIABLE DESCRIPTION	VAR (23)	VAR (24)	VAR (25)	VAR (26)	VAR (37)	VAR (38)	VAR (39)
VAR(1)	0.378*	0.639	-0.126	-0.002	-0.075	-0.055	0.292**
VAR(2)	-0.280	0.132	-0.103	0.180	-0.125	-0.190*	-0.044
VAR(3)	-0.228	-0.712	0.306**	0.143	0.435***	-0.331***	0.215*
VAR(4)	-0.248	-0.424	0.099	0.164	-0.034	-0.043	0.218*
VAR(5)	0.065	-0.352	0.037	0.085	0.157	0.076	0.251**
VAR(6)	0.352	-0.252	-0.085	0.010	0.333***	0.350***	0.395***
VAR(7)	0.195	-0.470	-0.074	0.018	0.350***	0.321***	0.291**
VAR(10)	-0.194	-0.423	0.022	0.031	-0.054	0.013	0.115
VAR(11)	-0.143	-0.649	0.341**	0.194	0.186	0.167	-0.046
VAR(12)	-0.225	-0.676	-0.084	0.255**	-0.109	-0.035	0.073
VAR(13)	-0.465**	-0.837	-0.107	0.239*	-0.052	-0.061	0.179
VAR(14)	-0.308	-0.802	0.321***	-0.239*	0.036	0.004	-0.230*
VAR(15)	-0.152	0.755	-0.200*	-0.067	0.168	0.209*	0.412***
VAR(16)	-0.117	-0.919	0.185	0.208*	0.080	0.084	-0.044
VAR(17)	-0.100	0.925	-0.098	0.016	0.239*	0.338***	0.156
VAR(18)	0.138	-0.380	-0.095	0.149	0.271**	0.115	0.322***
VAR(19)	-0.280	-0.871	-0.195*	0.175	-0.045	-0.125	0.241*
VAR(20)	-0.049	-0.941	0.365***	0.069	0.282**	0.350***	-0.092
VAR(21)	-0.268	-0.422	0.418***	0.134	-0.103	0.195*	-0.226*
VAR(22)	0.349	0.945	-0.182	-0.541***	-0.200	-0.116	0.185
VAR(23)	1.000	0.911	-0.094	-0.398*	0.052	0.123	0.251
VAR(24)	0.911	1.000	-0.529	-0.881	0.587	0.950	0.742
VAR(25)	-0.094	-0.529	1.000	0.141	0.151	0.325***	-0.331***
VAR(26)	-0.398*	-0.881	0.141	1.000	-0.143	-0.167	-0.134
VAR(37)	0.052	0.587	0.151	-0.143	1.000	0.744***	0.097
VAR(38)	0.123	0.950	0.325***	-0.167	0.744***	1.000	-0.074
VAR(39)	0.251	0.742	-0.331***	-0.134	0.097	-0.074	1.000

Table A-3
Correlation Matrix of Harvard Reviewers' Responses

CORRELATION COEFFICIENTS

VARIABLE DESCRIPTION	VAR (1)	VAR (2)	VAR (3)	VAR (4)	VAR (5)	VAR (6)	VAR (7)	VAR (8)	VAR (9)	VAR (10)
VAR(1)	1.000	-0.084	0.038	0.105	-0.132	-0.058	-0.049	0.048	0.034	-0.027
VAR(2)	-0.084	1.000	-0.034	-0.048	0.206*	0.033	0.096	-0.086	-0.112	-0.173
VAR(3)	0.038	-0.034	1.000	0.561***	0.405***	0.237*	0.351***	0.431***	0.405***	0.040
VAR(4)	0.105	-0.048	0.561***	1.000	0.353***	0.356***	0.456***	0.378**	0.376**	0.409*
VAR(5)	-0.132	0.206*	0.405***	0.353***	1.000	0.311**	0.161	0.102	0.046	0.141
VAR(6)	-0.058	0.033	0.237*	0.356***	0.311**	1.000	0.567***	0.458**	0.416***	-0.014
VAR(7)	-0.049	0.096	0.351***	0.456***	0.161	0.567***	1.000	0.779***	0.762***	0.397**
VAR(8)	0.048	-0.086	0.431***	0.378**	0.102	0.458***	0.779***	1.000	0.965***	0.589***
VAR(9)	0.034	-0.112	0.405***	0.376**	0.046	0.416***	0.762***	0.965***	1.000	0.536***
VAR(10)	-0.027	-0.173	0.040	0.409*	0.141	-0.014	0.397**	0.589***	0.536***	1.000
VAR(11)	0.078	0.202	0.391*	0.397*	-0.367*	0.445**	0.192	0.295	0.247	-0.026
VAR(12)	0.064	0.294**	0.011	0.034	-0.015	0.303**	0.320**	0.294*	0.312**	-0.001
VAR(13)	0.041	0.265**	0.170	0.194	-0.097	0.072	0.254*	0.278*	0.271*	0.215
VAR(14)	0.007	-0.017	0.286**	0.286*	0.142	0.025	0.124	0.283*	0.211	0.079
VAR(15)	-0.091	0.078	0.128	0.211	0.256**	0.476***	0.367***	0.254*	0.192	0.176
VAR(16)	-0.014	0.090	0.387***	0.246*	0.168	0.043	0.191	0.245*	0.247*	-0.051
VAR(17)	0.109	0.160	0.234*	0.210	0.342***	0.310**	0.324**	0.227	0.277*	0.298*
VAR(18)	0.120	0.143	0.259**	0.327**	0.332***	0.344***	0.304**	0.321**	0.284*	0.157
VAR(19)	-0.079	0.237*	0.016	0.228*	0.253**	0.231*	0.235*	0.152	0.169	0.235
VAR(20)	-0.037	-0.070	0.458***	0.173	0.098	0.220*	0.354***	0.254*	0.250*	0.015
VAR(21)	-0.262	-0.044	0.272**	0.244*	0.010	0.081	0.210	0.206	0.232	0.095
VAR(22)	0.447*	-0.399	-0.199	-0.235	0.133	0.204	0.223	0.159	0.143	-0.404
VAR(23)	0.821	-0.410*	-0.040	-0.052	0.300	0.322	0.228	-0.002	-0.099	-0.262
VAR(24)	-0.217*	0.0	-0.856	-0.803	-0.115	-0.430	-0.695	-1.000*	-0.981	0.0
VAR(25)	-0.044	-0.087	0.297***	0.148	-0.113	-0.000	0.049	0.107	0.188	-0.078
VAR(26)	-0.063	-0.306**	0.153	0.220	-0.183	-0.015	0.019	0.064	0.054	-0.164
VAR(27)	-0.114	-0.028	0.138	0.064	0.082	-0.031	-0.115	0.003	-0.031	-0.165
VAR(28)	-0.008	0.048	0.370***	0.087	-0.301**	0.191	0.146	0.170	-0.105	-0.238
VAR(29)	-0.044	0.150	0.438***	0.244*	-0.019	0.348***	0.344***	0.137	0.088	-0.101
VAR(30)	-0.044	0.167	0.119	0.164	0.199*	0.322**	0.289**	0.001	0.019	-0.250
VAR(31)	-0.082	0.044	0.244*	0.057	-0.084	0.146	0.204*	0.238*	0.172	-0.042
VAR(32)	-0.066	0.042	0.064	0.093	0.155	-0.157	0.034	0.197	0.147	-0.205
VAR(33)	-0.079	0.233*	0.008	0.148	-0.184	0.184	0.194	0.203	0.086	0.364**
VAR(34)	-0.016	-0.054	0.006	-0.260*	-0.184	-0.099	-0.105	-0.145	-0.176	-0.191
VAR(35)	0.053	-0.136	0.103	-0.003	-0.128	-0.209*	-0.113	-0.106	-0.124	-0.251
VAR(36)	-0.056	-0.006	0.134	0.152	-0.001	0.055	0.121	0.258*	-0.280*	0.187
VAR(37)	-0.069	-0.053	0.512***	0.274*	0.219*	0.361***	0.319**	0.234*	0.320**	-0.008
VAR(38)	-0.046	-0.092	0.416***	0.179	0.194	0.315**	0.327**	0.163	0.221	0.070
VAR(39)	0.160	-0.013	0.382***	0.414***	0.338***	0.352***	0.353***	0.166	0.138	0.196

Table A-3 (cont.)

CORRELATION COEFFICIENTS

VARIABLE DESCRIPTION	VAR (11)	VAR (12)	VAR (13)	VAR (14)	VAR (15)	VAR (16)	VAR (17)	VAR (18)	VAR (19)	VAR (20)
VAR(1)	0.078	0.064	0.041	0.007	-0.091	-0.014	-0.251*	0.109	0.120	-0.079
VAR(2)	0.202	0.294**	0.265**	-0.017	0.078	0.090	0.160	0.143	0.237*	-0.070
VAR(3)	0.391*	0.011	0.170	0.286**	0.128	0.387***	0.234*	0.259**	0.016	0.458***
VAR(4)	0.397*	0.034	0.194	0.286*	0.211	0.246*	0.210	0.327**	0.228*	0.173
VAR(5)	-0.367*	-0.015	-0.097	0.142	0.256***	0.168	0.342***	0.332***	-0.253***	0.098
VAR(6)	-0.445**	0.303**	0.072	0.025	0.476***	0.043	0.310**	0.344***	0.231*	0.220*
VAR(7)	0.192	0.320*	0.254*	0.124	0.367***	0.191	0.324***	0.304**	0.235*	0.354***
VAR(8)	0.255	0.294*	0.278*	0.283*	0.254*	0.245*	0.227	0.321*	0.152	0.254*
VAR(9)	0.347	0.312**	0.271*	0.211	0.152	0.247*	0.277*	0.284*	0.169	0.250*
VAR(10)	-0.026	-0.001	0.215	0.079	0.176	0.051	0.298*	0.157	0.235	0.015
VAR(11)	1.000	0.172	0.103	0.311	0.225	0.361	0.336*	0.150	0.235	0.259
VAR(12)	0.172	1.000	0.491***	0.108	0.201*	0.189*	0.179	0.270*	0.114	0.106
VAR(13)	0.103	0.491***	1.000	0.035	0.154	0.150	0.171	0.150	0.124	0.327***
VAR(14)	0.311	0.108	0.035	1.000	-0.065	0.672***	-0.110	0.420***	0.045	0.194*
VAR(15)	0.225	0.201*	0.154	-0.065	1.000	-0.141	0.542***	0.336***	0.058	0.290**
VAR(16)	0.361*	0.189*	0.150	0.672***	-0.141	1.000	-0.119	0.237*	0.017	0.243*
VAR(17)	0.336*	0.270**	0.171	-0.110	0.542***	-0.119	1.000	0.154	0.185	0.304**
VAR(18)	-0.421**	0.114	0.151	0.420***	0.386***	0.237*	0.185	1.000	0.217***	0.158
VAR(19)	0.259	0.124	0.124	0.045	0.058	0.017	0.154	0.138	1.000	-0.225*
VAR(20)	-0.169	0.106	0.327***	0.194*	0.108	0.243*	0.304**	-0.338***	-0.225*	1.000
VAR(21)	-0.295	0.249*	0.244*	0.517***	0.290**	0.516***	-0.028	-0.558	-0.159	-0.247
VAR(22)	-0.045	-0.543*	-0.413	-0.395	0.089	-0.188	-0.079	-0.133	-0.423	-0.303
VAR(23)	0.0	-0.289	-0.352	-0.202	0.188	-0.051	0.992	-0.050	-0.990	-0.761
VAR(24)	-0.330*	-0.940	-0.974	-0.997	0.965	-0.976	-0.076	0.132	-0.637	-0.341***
VAR(25)	0.093	-0.041	-0.073	0.312***	-0.185	0.189*	0.205*	0.166	-0.219*	-0.046
VAR(26)	0.125	0.218*	0.157	0.222*	-0.016	0.246*	-0.002	0.054	-0.203*	0.355***
VAR(27)	0.296	0.029	-0.104	0.265*	-0.095	0.200*	0.068	-0.204*	-0.047	0.382***
VAR(28)	0.202	0.063	0.051	0.216*	0.018	0.273*	0.153	0.240*	-0.147	0.270**
VAR(29)	0.045	0.097	0.120	0.125	0.315***	0.174	0.345***	0.292**	-0.076	0.356***
VAR(30)	0.267	0.192*	0.179	-0.038	0.304*	0.140	0.118	-0.148	0.012	0.085
VAR(31)	-0.039	0.371***	0.276***	0.292**	0.030	0.345***	0.223*	0.174	0.009	0.182
VAR(32)	-0.145	0.168	0.203*	0.312***	-0.052	0.276***	-0.043	-0.030	-0.130	0.256**
VAR(33)	-0.003	0.208*	0.214*	-0.196*	0.657***	-0.246*	0.539***	-0.065	-0.205*	0.285**
VAR(34)	-0.047	0.133	0.140	-0.163	0.089	-0.220*	0.172	0.040	0.297*	0.221*
VAR(35)	0.282	0.092	-0.027	-0.013	0.207*	0.053	-0.064	0.364***	-0.206*	0.440***
VAR(36)	0.379*	0.136	0.158	0.327***	0.037	0.345***	0.077	0.252*	-0.154	0.435***
VAR(37)	0.211	-0.050	0.030	0.033	0.157	0.057	0.355***	0.258*	-0.037	0.223*
VAR(38)		0.044	0.014	-0.002	0.276**	0.016	0.452***		-0.160	
VAR(39)		0.046	0.198*	-0.031	0.444***	-0.010	0.195*		-0.129	

Table A-3 (cont.)

CORRELATION COEFFICIENTS

VARIABLE DESCRIPTION	VAR (21)	VAR (22)	VAR (23)	VAR (24)	VAR (25)	VAR (26)	VAR (27)	VAR (28)	VAR (29)	VAR (30)
VAR(1)	-0.037	0.262	0.447*	0.821	-0.217*	-0.044	-0.063	-0.114	-0.008	-0.044
VAR(2)	-0.044	-0.399	-0.410*	0.0	-0.087	0.306***	-0.028	0.048	0.150	0.044
VAR(3)	0.272**	-0.199	-0.040	-0.803	0.297***	0.153	0.138	0.370***	0.438***	-0.119
VAR(4)	0.244*	0.235	-0.052	0.115	0.148	0.220	0.064	0.087	0.244*	0.164
VAR(5)	0.010	0.133	0.300	0.115	0.113	0.183	0.082	0.151	0.301**	-0.019
VAR(6)	0.081	0.204	0.322	-0.430	0.000	-0.015	-0.031	0.191	0.348***	0.322**
VAR(7)	0.210*	0.223	0.228	-0.695	0.049	0.019	-0.115	0.146	0.344***	0.289**
VAR(8)	0.206	0.159	-0.002	-1.000*	0.107	0.064	-0.003	0.170	0.137	0.001
VAR(9)	0.232	0.143	0.099	0.981	0.188	0.054	-0.031	0.105	0.088	0.019
VAR(10)	0.095	0.404	-0.262	0.0	0.078	-0.164	-0.165	-0.238	-0.101	-0.250
VAR(11)	0.169	-0.295	-0.045	-0.940	0.330*	0.093	0.125	0.296	-0.202	-0.045
VAR(12)	0.249**	-0.543*	-0.289	-0.974	-0.041	0.218*	0.029	0.063	0.097	0.192*
VAR(13)	0.244*	-0.413	-0.352	-0.997*	-0.073	0.157	-0.104	0.051	0.120	-0.179
VAR(14)	0.617***	-0.395	-0.202	-0.997*	0.312***	-0.222*	0.265**	0.216*	0.315***	0.304***
VAR(15)	0.108	0.089	-0.051	0.965	-0.185	-0.016	-0.095	0.018	0.174	0.140
VAR(16)	0.516***	-0.188	0.188	0.976	0.189*	0.246**	0.200*	0.273**	0.345***	-0.118
VAR(17)	-0.028	-0.079	-0.051	0.992	0.205*	-0.002	0.068	0.153	0.204*	0.240*
VAR(18)	0.338***	-0.558*	0.133	0.837	-0.050	0.132	0.166	0.054	0.076	0.012
VAR(19)	-0.159	-0.423	-0.411*	0.990	0.219*	0.203*	-0.047	-0.147	-0.382***	0.270**
VAR(20)	0.484***	-0.247	0.302	-0.761	0.341***	-0.046	0.046	0.355***	0.121	0.174
VAR(21)	1.000	0.058	-0.142	-0.930	-0.158	-0.040	0.292**	0.287**	0.041	0.252
VAR(22)	0.058	1.000	0.247	0.918	-0.557*	-0.557*	0.085	0.096	0.396*	0.543***
VAR(23)	-0.142	0.247	1.000	0.992	-0.145	-0.603***	0.011	0.172	0.814	0.115
VAR(24)	-0.930	0.918	0.992	1.000	-0.742	-1.000*	-0.963	-0.734	0.238*	-0.067
VAR(25)	-0.158	-0.557*	-0.145	-0.742	1.000	-0.007	0.489***	0.414***	0.219*	0.324***
VAR(26)	-0.040	-0.557*	-0.603***	-1.000*	-0.007	1.000	0.151	0.051	0.151	0.045
VAR(27)	0.292**	0.085	0.011	-0.963	0.489***	0.151	1.000	0.482***	0.219*	-0.009
VAR(28)	0.287**	0.096	0.172	-0.734	0.414***	0.051	0.482***	1.000	0.595***	0.244*
VAR(29)	0.041	0.396*	0.814	0.238*	0.219*	0.151	0.219*	0.595***	1.000	0.373***
VAR(30)	0.252	0.543***	0.115	-0.067	0.324***	0.045	-0.009	0.244*	0.373***	1.000
VAR(31)	0.352***	0.252	0.158	-0.995	0.030	0.339***	0.363***	0.364***	-0.120	-0.103
VAR(32)	-0.234*	-0.631*	-0.304	0.948	-0.238*	0.084	-0.155	-0.009	0.088	0.037
VAR(33)	-0.080	0.099	-0.301	-0.115	0.113	-0.184	-0.109	-0.162	0.119	-0.009
VAR(34)	0.100	0.184	-0.247	0.838	0.076	-0.123	-0.056	0.191*	0.287**	0.287**
VAR(35)	0.129	0.130	0.282	-0.160	0.152	-0.010	0.016	0.068	0.119	-0.009
VAR(36)	0.318***	0.230	0.380	0.855	0.191	-0.062	0.091	0.008	0.287**	0.435***
VAR(37)	0.169	-0.296	0.114	0.987	0.191	-0.190	0.093	0.235*	0.433***	0.103
VAR(38)	-0.225*	-0.094	0.332	0.987	0.370***	-0.190	0.093	0.323***	0.510***	0.331***
VAR(39)	-0.042	0.031	0.391*	0.818	-0.191*	-0.037	-0.254**	-0.065	0.288***	0.227*

Table A-3 (cont.)

CORRELATION COEFFICIENTS

VARIABLE DESCRIPTION	VAR (31)	VAR (32)	VAR (33)	VAR (34)	VAR (35)	VAR (36)	VAR (37)	VAR (38)	VAR (39)
VAR(1)	-C.C82	0.066	-0.079	-0.016	0.053	-0.056	-0.069	-0.046	C.160
VAR(2)	C.167	0.042	0.233*	-C.054	-C.136	-0.006	-0.053	-0.092	-0.013
VAR(3)	0.244*	0.064	0.008	0.006	-0.103	0.134	0.512***	0.416***	C.382***
VAR(4)	C.C57	0.093	0.148	-0.260*	-0.003	0.152	0.274*	0.179	C.414**
VAR(5)	0.199*	-0.084	0.155	-C.184	-C.128	-0.001	0.219*	0.194	0.38***
VAR(6)	0.14b	-0.157	0.184	-0.099	0.209*	0.055	0.361***	0.315**	C.352***
VAR(7)	C.204*	0.034	0.194	-0.105	-0.113	0.121	0.319***	0.327***	C.353***
VAR(8)	C.238*	0.197	0.203	-0.145	-C.106	0.258*	0.234*	0.163	C.166
VAR(9)	C.172	0.147	0.086	-0.176	-0.124	0.280*	0.320**	0.221	C.138
VAR(10)	-0.042	0.205	0.364**	-C.191	-C.251	0.187	-0.008	0.070	0.196
VAR(11)	C.207	0.267	0.039	-C.145	-0.092	0.047	0.282	0.379*	C.211
VAR(12)	C.371***	C.168	0.208*	-C.133	-0.092	0.136	-0.050	0.044	0.046
VAR(13)	0.276***	0.203*	0.214*	C.140	-0.027	0.158	0.030	0.014	0.198*
VAR(14)	0.292***	0.312***	-0.196*	-0.163	-0.013	0.327***	0.033	-0.002	-C.C21
VAR(15)	-0.030	-0.052	0.657***	0.089	0.207*	0.037	0.157	0.276**	0.444***
VAR(16)	0.345***	-0.276**	-0.246**	-0.220*	-0.053	0.345***	0.057	0.016	-0.010
VAR(17)	0.223*	-C.043	0.539****	0.172	-0.064	0.077	0.355***	0.452***	C.195*
VAR(18)	C.292**	C.148	0.174	-C.030	-0.065	0.040	0.364***	0.252*	C.238*
VAR(19)	-0.009	C.130	0.205*	-0.297**	-0.206*	-0.154	-0.037	-0.160	C.129
VAR(20)	C.356***	-0.085	0.182	0.256**	0.285**	0.221*	0.440***	0.435***	-0.223*
VAR(21)	C.352***	0.234*	0.080	C.100	0.129	0.318***	0.169	0.235*	-0.042
VAR(22)	-C.297	-0.631*	-0.099	0.184	0.130	0.230	-0.296	-0.094	C.C21
VAR(23)	C.158	-0.304	0.301	-0.247	0.380	0.282	0.114	0.332	0.291*
VAR(24)	-C.760	0.995	0.948	-0.115	0.838	-0.160	0.855	0.987	C.818
VAR(25)	C.324***	-C.030	-0.238*	0.113	-0.076	0.152	0.191	0.370***	-0.191*
VAR(26)	0.045	0.339***	0.084	-C.184	-C.123	0.010	-0.062	-0.190	-0.037
VAR(27)	0.363***	0.125	-0.155	0.056	-0.109	0.016	0.091	0.093	-C.254*
VAR(28)	0.364***	-C.009	-0.162	0.191*	0.068	0.008	0.235*	0.323***	-0.065
VAR(29)	0.373***	0.170	0.088	C.119	0.287**	-0.141	0.433***	0.510***	-0.288*
VAR(30)	0.209*	-0.103	0.037	-0.009	0.435***	0.103	0.211*	0.331***	0.227*
VAR(31)	1.000	0.097	0.015	0.241*	0.004	0.157	0.301**	0.361***	-0.021
VAR(32)	0.097	1.000	0.033	-0.010	0.170	0.179	-0.069	-0.146	-0.091
VAR(33)	0.015	0.033	1.000	0.177	C.100	-0.036	0.075	0.081	0.263**
VAR(34)	C.241*	-C.010	0.177	1.000	-0.100	-0.036	0.272**	0.320**	-0.145
VAR(35)	C.004	0.177	-0.024	-0.100	1.000	0.059	0.093	0.253*	-C.C95
VAR(36)	C.157	-0.179	-0.036	-0.036	0.059	1.000	-0.161	-0.142	-C.156
VAR(37)	0.301**	-0.069	0.075	C.272**	0.253*	-0.142	1.000	0.782***	0.214*
VAR(38)	0.361***	-0.146	0.081	0.320**	0.095	-0.156	0.214*	1.000	C.C91
VAR(39)	-C.021	-0.091	0.263**	-C.145				1.000	

Table A-4

Correlation Matrix of Yugoslav Reviewers' Responses

CORRELATION COEFFICIENTS

VARIABLE DESCRIPTION	VAR (1)	VAR (2)	VAR (3)	VAR (4)	VAR (5)	VAR (6)	VAR (7)	VAR (8)	VAR (9)	VAR (10)
VAR(1)	1.000	-0.342***	0.146	C.251**	-0.219*	0.106	0.094	0.233*	0.274*	-0.244
VAR(2)	-C.342***	1.000	0.067	0.124	0.271**	0.124	-0.120	0.064	C.057	0.058
VAR(3)	0.146	0.067	1.000	0.582***	0.105	0.065	0.159	0.122	0.219	-0.097
VAR(4)	C.251**	0.124	0.582***	1.000	0.07C	0.015	0.055	-0.017	0.031	0.091
VAR(5)	-C.219*	0.271**	0.105	C.07C	1.000	0.155	0.123	0.027	0.087	0.199
VAR(6)	0.106	-C.124	0.065	0.015	0.155	1.000	0.553***	0.502***	C.422***	0.109
VAR(7)	C.094	-C.120	0.159	0.015	0.123	0.553***	1.000	0.408***	0.429***	0.124
VAR(8)	0.233*	0.064	0.122	-0.017	C.027	0.50C***	0.408***	1.000	0.912***	0.524***
VAR(9)	C.274*	0.058	0.219	0.031	0.087	0.422***	0.429***	0.912***	1.000	0.394*
VAR(10)	-0.244	0.058	-0.097	0.091	0.155	0.109	0.124	0.524***	0.394*	1.000
VAR(11)	-C.342*	0.087	0.219	0.065	0.214	-0.201	-0.018	-0.325	-0.148	-0.158
VAR(12)	-C.141	0.164	C.102	0.202*	-0.023	-0.007	-0.015	0.000	0.030	0.317
VAR(13)	-0.125	-0.154	-0.018	0.184	0.033	0.032	0.113	0.157	0.158	0.463***
VAR(14)	-C.086	-0.003	0.390***	C.309**	-0.073	-0.173	0.070	-0.328**	-0.311**	-0.168
VAR(15)	0.018	0.229*	-0.003	0.132	C.285**	0.334***	0.289**	0.285*	-0.237*	0.013
VAR(16)	-C.034	0.102	0.339***	0.238*	0.045	0.100	0.300*	-0.046	-0.049	0.074
VAR(17)	-C.031	0.227	0.106	0.024	0.60C***	0.267	0.447**	0.153	0.160	-0.548*
VAR(18)	0.012	0.181	0.032	0.156	0.161	0.142	0.264*	0.142	0.127	0.135
VAR(19)	0.214	0.165	-0.177	-0.669	0.273	0.031	0.171	-0.070	-0.042	-0.156
VAR(20)	-0.051	0.110	0.211*	0.148	0.389***	0.095	0.174	0.086	0.175	-0.079
VAR(21)	0.073	0.120	0.343***	0.347***	-0.086	-0.033	-0.093	-0.001	0.032	0.002
VAR(22)	-0.269	-0.379	-0.385	-0.414*	-0.116	-0.069	-0.056	-0.118	-0.189	-0.048
VAR(23)	-C.151	C.098	-0.618*	-0.613*	-0.007	0.361	-0.555	-0.720*	-0.549	-0.578
VAR(24)	-1.000	1.000	-1.000	1.000	-1.CCC	1.000	-1.000	-1.000	-1.000	-1.000
VAR(25)	C.137	-0.034	0.107	0.058	0.086	-0.023	-0.016	-0.290*	-0.215	-0.208
VAR(26)	C.031	C.032	C.108	0.193*	0.046	0.095	0.036	0.069	0.120	0.209
VAR(27)	-0.050	C.056	0.137	0.390	0.036	0.064	0.192	-0.092	-0.056	0.098
VAR(28)	-C.00⁵	0.252*	0.040	0.145	0.194	0.222	0.156	0.161	0.169	-0.319
VAR(29)	-0.044	0.254*	0.099	0.073	C.321**	0.168	0.266*	0.129	0.183	-0.162
VAR(30)	C.020	0.102	0.084	0.123	-0.061	0.181	0.084	0.009	0.027	-0.325
VAR(31)	C.069	-C.092	C.212	0.145	-C.065	-0.023	0.290*	-0.171	-0.227	-0.240
VAR(32)	0.174	-C.271*	-0.005	0.068	0.378**	-0.163	0.020	-0.151	-0.166	-0.000
VAR(33)	-C.039	C.290*	0.087	0.113	0.253*	0.128	0.130	0.325**	0.286**	-0.010
VAR(34)	-0.00C	0.078	0.011	0.048	0.300**	0.241*	0.132	0.178	0.117	-0.206
VAR(35)	C.028	-0.046	-0.059	-0.120	0.285**	0.269*	0.306**	0.210	0.230	-0.012
VAR(36)	0.097	-0.142	0.126	C.15C	0.133	-0.146	0.065	0.175	0.109	-0.141
VAR(37)	-0.036	-0.066	0.206*	0.022	0.081	0.137	0.173	0.105	C.160	-0.223
VAR(38)	C.050	-0.117	0.155	0.130	0.075	0.120	0.115	0.023	0.022	-0.347*
VAR(39)	C.527***	-0.067	0.006	0.123	-0.072	0.042	-0.024	0.170	0.150	-0.109

Table A-4 (cont.)

CORRELATION COEFFICIENTS

VARIABLE DESCRIPTION	VAR (11)	VAR (12)	VAR (13)	VAR (14)	VAR (15)	VAR (16)	VAR (17)	VAR (18)	VAR (19)	VAR (20)
VAR(1)	-0.342*	-0.141	-0.125	-0.086	0.018	-0.034	-0.031	0.012	0.214	-0.051
VAR(2)	0.087	0.164	0.154	-0.003	0.229*	0.102	0.227	0.181	0.165	0.110
VAR(3)	0.219	0.102	-0.018	0.390***	-0.003	0.336**	0.106	0.032	-0.177	0.211*
VAR(4)	0.065	0.202*	0.184	0.309***	0.132	0.238*	0.024	0.156	-0.069	0.148
VAR(5)	0.214	-0.023	0.033	-0.073	0.285**	0.045	0.600***	0.161	0.273	0.389***
VAR(6)	-0.201	-0.007	0.032	-0.173	0.334***	0.100	0.267	0.142	0.031	0.095
VAR(7)	-0.018	0.015	0.113	0.070	0.289**	0.300*	0.447***	0.264**	0.171	0.174
VAR(8)	-0.325	0.000	0.157	-0.328**	0.285*	-0.046	0.153	0.142	-0.070	0.086
VAR(9)	-0.148	0.030	0.158	-0.311**	0.237*	-0.049	0.160	0.127	-0.042	0.175
VAR(10)	-0.158	0.317	0.463**	-0.169	0.013	0.074	-0.548*	-0.135	-0.156	-0.079
VAR(11)	1.000	0.329	0.287	0.062	0.204	-0.014	0.071	-0.262	-0.157	0.151
VAR(12)	0.329	1.000	0.425***	0.237**	0.172	0.327**	-0.013	-0.215*	0.009	0.082
VAR(13)	0.287	0.425***	1.000	0.206**	0.156	0.289*	0.119	0.121	0.253	0.199*
VAR(14)	0.062	0.237*	0.206**	1.000	-0.168	0.514***	0.181	0.030	0.154	0.266**
VAR(15)	-0.204	0.172	0.156	-0.168	1.000	0.145	0.522***	0.342***	0.056	0.126
VAR(16)	-0.014	0.327**	0.289*	0.514***	0.145	1.000	0.258	0.167	0.553***	0.270*
VAR(17)	0.071	-0.013	0.119	0.181	0.522***	0.258	1.000	0.133	0.553***	0.603***
VAR(18)	-0.262	0.215*	0.121	0.030	0.342***	0.167	0.133	1.000	0.311	0.005
VAR(19)	-0.151	0.082	0.199*	0.266**	0.056	0.553***	0.553***	0.311	1.000	0.337
VAR(20)	-0.133	0.217*	0.207*	0.538***	-0.005	0.442***	0.603***	0.005	0.337	1.000
VAR(21)	-0.328	0.117	0.088	-0.244	-0.050	0.012	0.118	0.154	0.080	-0.299**
VAR(22)	-0.062	-0.095	-0.529	-0.290	0.072	-0.012	-0.231	0.250	-0.084	-0.214
VAR(23)	-1.000	-1.000	-1.000	-1.000	-1.000	-0.461	-0.986*	-0.306	-0.006	-0.208
VAR(24)	-0.185	-0.011	-0.117	0.195*	-0.046	0.0	0.149	-1.000	0.0	-1.000
VAR(25)	-0.135	0.115	0.264*	0.218**	0.041	0.097	0.036	0.064	0.164	0.185
VAR(26)	-0.077	0.109	-0.087	0.306**	0.080	0.213	-0.003	-0.011	0.093	0.248*
VAR(27)	0.419*	-0.147	0.046	-0.137	0.271*	0.247	0.086	0.303**	0.322	-0.096
VAR(28)	-0.379*	-0.175	-0.042	-0.258*	0.352***	-0.068	0.418**	0.154	-0.248	-0.012
VAR(29)	0.303	0.120	0.146	0.018	0.052	-0.018	0.367*	0.238*	-0.121	0.121
VAR(30)	0.238	0.172	0.064	0.389**	-0.001	-0.115	0.105	0.220	-0.012	0.068
VAR(31)	-0.205	0.155	0.253	0.164	0.029	0.526***	0.105	0.155	0.474	0.012
VAR(32)	-0.051	0.210*	0.383***	-0.044	0.508***	0.276	-0.433	0.072	0.402	-0.299*
VAR(33)	-0.154	0.057	0.053	-0.110	0.346**	0.212	0.303*	0.458***	0.230	0.168
VAR(34)	-0.125	-0.076	0.090	-0.269*	0.181	0.090	0.297	0.315**	0.212	0.102
VAR(35)	-0.166	0.128	0.114	0.181	0.296**	0.073	0.303	0.185	-0.061	-0.089
VAR(36)	-0.169	-0.071	-0.087	-0.110	0.269**	-0.280*	0.525***	0.291***	0.248	0.303**
VAR(37)	-0.026	-0.148	-0.150	-0.033	0.081	-0.068	0.313*	0.098	0.046	0.036
VAR(38)	-0.322	0.044	0.011	-0.031	0.059	0.025	0.462**	0.071	0.284	0.086
VAR(39)					0.059	0.016	0.105	0.090	0.389*	-0.119

Table A-4 (cont.)

CORRELATION COEFFICIENTS

VARIABLE DESCRIPTION	VAR (21)	VAR (22)	VAR (23)	VAR (24)	VAR (25)	VAR (26)	VAR (27)	VAR (28)	VAR (29)	VAR (30)
VAR(1)	C.073	0.269	-0.151	-1.000	0.137	0.C31	-0.C50	-0.C05	-0.044	0.020
VAR(2)	0.120	-C.379	0.098	1.00C	-0.034	0.032	0.056	0.252*	0.256*	0.102
VAR(3)	C.343***	-0.385	-C.618*	-1.000	0.107	0.108	0.137	0.040	0.099	0.084
VAR(4)	C.347***	-0.414*	-0.613*	-1.000	0.058	0.193*	0.090	0.145	0.073	-0.123
VAR(5)	0.086	-0.116	-0.007	-1.00C	0.C86	0.046	-0.036	0.194	0.321**	-0.061
VAR(6)	-0.033	-0.069	0.361	1.000	-0.023	0.095	0.064	0.222	0.168	0.181
VAR(7)	0.093	-0.C56	-0.555	-1.000	-0.016	0.036	0.192	0.156	0.266*	0.084
VAR(8)	-0.001	-0.118	-0.720*	-1.000	-0.250*	0.069	-0.092	0.161	0.129	0.009
VAR(9)	-0.032	-0.189	-0.549	-1.000	-0.215	0.120	-0.096	0.169	0.183	-0.027
VAR(10)	-0.002	-0.048	-0.578	-1.000	-0.2C9	0.20S	0.098	-0.319	-0.162	-0.325
VAR(11)	C.133	-0.328	-0.062	-1.000	0.185	0.135	-0.077	0.419*	0.379*	-0.303
VAR(12)	0.217*	0.117	-0.095	-1.00C	-0.011	0.109	0.109	-0.147	-0.175	0.120
VAR(13)	C.207**	0.088	0.529	-1.000	-0.117	0.264**	-0.087	0.046	-0.042	0.146
VAR(14)	C.538***	-0.244	-0.290	-1.000	-0.195*	0.218*	0.306**	-0.137	-0.258*	0.018
VAR(15)	-0.005	-0.050	0.072	1.000	-0.046	0.041	0.08C	0.271*	0.352***	0.052
VAR(16)	C.442***	0.012	-0.461	0.0	0.C97	0.247	0.C68	-0.068	-0.018	0.115
VAR(17)	C.118	-0.231	-0.986*	C.0	0.145	0.036	-0.003	0.086	0.418**	0.367*
VAR(18)	0.154	0.250	-0.306	1.000	0.064	-0.011	0.303**	0.154	0.238*	0.220
VAR(19)	0.080	-0.084	0.006	0.0	0.164	0.093	0.322	-0.248	-0.121	0.012
VAR(20)	C.290***	-0.214	-0.208	-1.000	0.185	0.248*	-0.096	-0.012	0.121	0.068
VAR(21)	1.000	0.134	-C.276	1.00C	0.277***	0.266***	0.166	0.039	0.021	0.103
VAR(22)	C.134	1.000	0.489	0.0	-0.318	-0.547***	-0.122	-0.349	-0.444	-0.008
VAR(23)	-0.276	0.489	1.00C	C.0	0.31S	-0.182	0.246	-0.309	-0.005	0.189
VAR(24)	1.000	0.0	0.0	1.000	0.C	-1.000	1.00C	1.000	1.000	0.0
VAR(25)	C.277**	-0.318	-0.319	0.0	1.000	0.293**	0.207	-0.045	0.184	0.088
VAR(26)	C.266**	-0.547***	-0.182	-1.000	0.253**	1.000	0.082	-0.097	-0.003	0.103
VAR(27)	C.166	-0.122	0.246	1.000	0.207	0.082	1.000	0.216	0.309**	0.334**
VAR(28)	0.039	-0.349	-0.309	1.000	-0.045	-0.097	0.216	1.000	0.576***	0.279*
VAR(29)	C.021	-0.444	-0.005	0.0	0.184	-0.003	0.30S**	0.576***	1.000	0.400***
VAR(30)	C.103	-0.008	0.189	0.0	0.C88	0.103	0.334**	0.279*	0.40C***	1.000
VAR(31)	C.299*	-0.030	-0.376	0.0	0.185	-0.044	0.453***	0.275	0.214	0.148
VAR(32)	C.164	0.086	-0.428	0.0	0.C05	0.170	0.263	-0.001	-0.057	0.065
VAR(33)	0.034	0.348	0.00C	0.0	-0.101	-0.151	0.171	0.290*	0.217*	0.137
VAR(34)	-C.037	0.225	0.179	0.0	0.086	-0.272*	0.084	0.135	0.226*	0.266*
VAR(35)	-C.048	0.076	0.003	-1.000	0.110	0.104	0.034	0.222	0.460***	0.422***
VAR(36)	C.267**	0.389	0.131	1.000	0.154	-0.089	0.213	0.021	0.033	0.175
VAR(37)	-C.224*	-0.249	-0.266	1.000	0.038	-0.208*	-0.039	0.112	0.153	-0.028
VAR(38)	-0.077	-0.003	-0.004	1.000	0.052	-0.107	0.035	0.042	0.045	0.055
VAR(39)	C.009	0.182	-0.423	-1.000	0.023	-0.065	-0.188	-0.165	-C.145	-0.025

174

Table A-4 (cont.)

CORRELATION COEFFICIENTS

VARIABLE DESCRIPTION	VAR (31)	VAR (32)	VAR (33)	VAR (34)	VAR (35)	VAR (36)	VAR (37)	VAR (38)	VAR (39)
VAR(1)	0.069	0.174	-0.035	-0.009	0.028	0.097	-0.036	0.050	0.527***
VAR(2)	-0.092	-0.271*	0.280**	0.078	-0.046	0.142	-0.066	-0.117	-0.067
VAR(3)	0.212	-0.005	0.087	0.011	-0.055	0.126	0.206*	0.155	0.006
VAR(4)	-0.145	0.068	0.113	0.048	-0.120	0.150	0.022	0.130	-0.123
VAR(5)	-0.069	-0.378***	0.253*	0.300**	0.285**	0.133	0.081	0.075	-0.072
VAR(6)	-0.023	-0.163	0.128	0.241*	0.265*	0.146	0.137	0.120	-0.042
VAR(7)	-0.290*	0.020	0.130	0.132	0.306**	0.065	0.173	0.115	-0.024
VAR(8)	-0.171	-0.151	0.325**	0.178	0.210	0.175	0.105	0.023	0.170
VAR(9)	-0.227	-0.166	0.286*	0.117	0.230	0.109	0.160	0.022	0.150
VAR(10)	-0.240	0.000	-0.010	-0.206	-0.012	-0.141	-0.223	-0.347*	-0.109
VAR(11)	-0.238	-0.205	-0.051	-0.154	-0.125	-0.169	0.166	0.026	-0.322
VAR(12)	0.172	0.155	0.210*	0.067	-0.076	0.128	-0.071	-0.148	-0.044
VAR(13)	0.064	0.253	0.383***	0.053	0.090	0.114	-0.087	-0.150	0.011
VAR(14)	0.389***	0.164	0.044	-0.110	-0.265*	0.181	-0.110	0.033	-0.031
VAR(15)	-0.001	0.229	0.508***	0.360**	0.181	0.296**	0.051	0.081	0.099
VAR(16)	0.526***	0.276	0.212	0.090	0.073	0.280*	-0.068	0.025	0.016
VAR(17)	0.105	-0.433	0.303*	0.297	0.303	0.525***	0.313*	0.462**	0.105
VAR(18)	0.155	0.072	0.458***	0.315**	0.185	0.291***	0.098	0.071	0.090
VAR(19)	0.474	0.402	0.230	0.212	-0.061	0.248	0.046	0.284	0.389*
VAR(20)	-0.012	-0.299*	0.168	0.037	0.089	0.303**	0.036	0.086	-0.119
VAR(21)	0.299*	0.164	0.034	-0.037	-0.048	0.267**	-0.224*	-0.077	-0.009
VAR(22)	-0.030	0.086	0.348	0.225	0.076	0.389	-0.249	-0.003	-0.182
VAR(23)	-0.376	-0.428	-0.000	0.179	0.003	0.131	-0.269	-0.004	-0.423
VAR(24)	0.0	0.005	0.0	0.0	-1.000	0.154	0.038	0.052	-0.023
VAR(25)	0.185	0.005	-0.101	0.086	0.110	0.085	-0.208*	-0.107	-0.065
VAR(26)	0.044	0.170	-0.151	-0.272*	0.104	0.213	-0.039	0.035	-0.188
VAR(27)	0.453***	-0.263	0.171	0.084	0.034	0.021	-0.112	0.042	-0.165
VAR(28)	0.275	-0.001	0.290*	0.135	0.222	0.033	0.193	0.045	-0.145
VAR(29)	0.214	-0.097	0.217*	0.226*	0.460***	0.175	0.028	0.055	-0.048
VAR(30)	0.148	0.065	0.137	0.266*	0.016	0.280*	-0.076	0.105	-0.025
VAR(31)	1.000	-0.544***	-0.047	0.364*	0.016	0.280*	0.076	0.105	0.048
VAR(32)	-0.544***	1.000	-0.039	-0.323*	-0.023	-0.008	-0.092	-0.070	0.261
VAR(33)	-0.047	-0.039	1.000	0.497***	0.129	0.282**	0.122	0.055	0.040
VAR(34)	0.364*	-0.323*	0.497***	1.000	0.326**	-0.040	0.112	0.042	0.023
VAR(35)	0.016	-0.023	0.129	0.326**	1.000	0.052	0.225*	0.102	-0.033
VAR(36)	0.280*	-0.008	0.282**	-0.040	0.052	1.000	0.226**	0.195	0.017
VAR(37)	0.076	-0.092	0.122	0.112	0.225*	0.226**	1.000	0.704***	-0.154
VAR(38)	0.105	-0.070	0.055	0.042	0.102	0.195	0.704***	1.000	-0.088
VAR(39)	0.048	0.261	0.040	0.023	-0.033	0.017	-0.154	-0.088	1.000

Table A-5

Summary of Publications Appearing to Date or Scheduled to Appear in Scientific or Professional Journals

Number of Articles	Number of Projects with Articles in			Total Articles
	English	Serbo-Croatian	Other	
0	87	95	109	0
1	7	8	1	16
2	1	3	0	8
3	3	0	0	9
4	2	2	0	16
5	1	1	0	10
6	4	0	0	24
7	1	0	0	7
8	1	0	0	8
.				
.				
.				
12	2	0	0	24
.				
.				
.				
28	0	1	0	28
.				
.				
.				
59	1	0	0	59
Total projects	110	110	110	209

Medical Student Questionnaire

Harvard Medical School
25 Shattuck Street
Boston, Massachusetts 02115
Regent 4-3300

Office of the Dean

This letter and the enclosed questionnaire are being sent to you as an American medical student who participated in the student exchange and spent a period of time in Yugoslavia. As you know, this program is being funded through counterpart funds, commonly known as P.L.-480 funds. The Office of the Secretary of Health, Education and Welfare has contracted with Harvard University to carry out an evaluation study on this P.L.-480 program in Yugoslavia.

The medical student fellowship program is an important component of that program, and we are very much interested in learning from you your reactions to your experience in Yugoslavia, and particularly how it has affected you and your future career as a physician. Your response to the enclosed questionnaire, which will be held confidential, will be of great help in making recommendations that may improve the program and make it a more meaningful experience for your younger colleagues. We are enclosing a stamped return envelope for your convenience. We sincerely hope you will cooperate in this endeavor that will take only a few minutes of your time.

Thank you.

Cordially yours,

Dieter Koch-Weser, M.D.
Associate Dean for
International Programs

Enc.

Questionnaire

Please answer each question of Part A, and, if you want to contribute to the future of the program, Part B. If the space provided is not sufficient, use the pages under C, identifying the number of each question.

Part A

1. Age (at the time you went to Yugoslavia)_____

   Sex: Male Female

   U.S. medical school at the time you went to Yugoslavia:

   Year of graduation:

   Present activity:

   Were you married at the time?

   Did your spouse accompany you?

2. Reasons for applying to the Program (check one or more)
   1. Study a different health care system
   2. Study disease and health conditions different from those in U.S.
   3. Get away from U.S. medical school routine
   4. Live in and learn from a different society and culture
   5. Other reasons. Please explain in as much detail as you wish.

3. Nature and quality of briefing received in the U.S.
   1. Very good
   2. Good
   3. Acceptable
   4. Non-acceptable
   5. No briefing
   6. Remarks (optional)

4. Who gave this briefing in the U.S. and when was it held?

5. Nature and quality of the Yugoslav formal briefing and reception:
   1. Very good
   2. Good
   3. Acceptable
   4. Non-acceptable
   5. No briefing
   6. Remarks (optional)

6. Who gave this briefing in Yugoslavia and when was it held?

7. Describe the types of living arrangements in Yugoslavia and how satisfactory they were.

   1. Very good
   2. Good
   3. Acceptable
   4. Non-acceptable
   5. Remarks (optional)

8. Did you write a formal report(s)?

   For whom?

   Has it been published?

9. Nature of your relationships with your Yugoslav preceptors and other Yugoslav faculty and professional staff.

   1. Very good
   2. Good
   3. Acceptable
   4. Non-acceptable
   5. Remarks (optional)

10. Nature of your relationships with your Yugoslav co-students.

   1. Very good
   2. Good
   3. Acceptable
   4. Non-acceptable
   5. Remarks (optional)

11. Nature of your relationships with the Yugoslav administrators of the program.

   1. Very good
   2. Good
   3. Acceptable
   4. Non-acceptable
   5. Remarks (optional)

12. Nature of additional significant contacts.

   1. Professional
   2. Others

13. (a) Did you speak one of the languages of Yugoslavia?

Which one?
Fluently?
Moderately well?
Little?

Remarks (optional)

(b) *If not*, was the lack of language knowledge an impediment?

Serious
Some
Little
None

Remarks (optional)

14. Was your activity in Yugoslavia primarily in

Basic Sciences?
Curative Medicine?
Preventive Medicine/Public Health/Community Health?
If other, what?

Remarks (optional)

15. (a) Did your activities in Yugoslavia change or influence your career plans?

Yes   No

Remarks (optional)

(b) What were your career plans before going to Yugoslavia?

(c) What were they after your return?

(d) What are they now?

(e) If your career plans are still the same, has your general outlook on medical care changed?

(f) Additional remarks (optional)

16. Which was your single most important medical experience in Yugoslavia?

17. Which was your single most important non-medical experience in Yugoslavia?

18. Would you rate your medical or your non-medical experience in Yugoslavia as more significant?

Medical   Non-Medical

Remarks

19. Was your experience in Yugoslavia

Much better than you expected?
Better than you expected?
About what you expected?
Less valuable than you expected?
Worthless?

Remarks (optional)

20. Was the experience of your spouse (if applicable) in Yugoslavia

Much better than she/he expected?
Better than she/he expected?
About what she/he expected?
Less valuable than she/he expected?
Worthless?

Remarks (optional)

Part B: Optional

If you are willing to spend a few more minutes, please comment on the following:

21. Do you have recommendations for future programs?

In relation to:

(a) Mechanism of selection of participants

(b) Financial aspects

(c) Preparation in the U.S.

(d) Preparation in Yugoslavia

(e) Professional program in Yugoslavia

(f) Non-professional activities in Yugoslavia

(g) Follow-up activities in the U.S.

(h) Other recommendation

Part C: Additional Remarks:

Index

About the Authors

Ralph E. Berry, Jr. is Professor of Economics at the Harvard School of Public Health and a member of the Faculty of the John F. Kennedy School of Government, Harvard University. He received the B.A. and M.A. from Boston University and the Ph.D. from Harvard University. He has been a consultant to many federal government agencies, to the National Hospital Institute of The Netherlands, and to the National Development Council of Argentina. Dr. Berry's major area of interest is health economics; he is the author of numerous articles concerning hospital services, costs, and structure, which have appeared in various professional journals.

Mark G. Field, a native of Switzerland, is Professor of Sociology at Boston University, Visiting Lecturer at the Harvard School of Public Health, and an Associate at the Russian Research Center, Harvard University. He has been associated with the Russian Research Center since its inception in 1948. He received the A.B. in sociology from Harvard College, the A.M. in regional studies (Soviet Union) and the Ph.D. in social relations (sociology) from Harvard University. Dr. Field is the author of two books on the Soviet health system and many articles appearing in sociological and medical journals. His major interests are the sociology of medicine and health (physical and mental), comparative social institutions, and contemporary Soviet society.

John A. Karefa-Smart is Visiting Professor of International Health at the Harvard Medical School and the Harvard School of Public Health. A native of Sierra Leone, he once served as that country's first foreign minister; later he was Assistant Director General of the World Health Organization in Geneva. Dr. Karefa-Smart is a graduate of McGill University Medical School and the Harvard School of Public Health. He has received honorary LL.D's from McGill University, Boston University, and Otterbein College.

Dieter Koch-Weser is an internist and Associate Dean of Harvard Medical School. He is responsible for administering the International Medical Programs of the school; he also teaches in the Department of Preventive and Social Medicine. Born and educated in Germany, Dr. Koch-Weser studied and practiced medicine in Brazil, and has done research in experimental pathology and taught at the University of Chicago and Western Reserve University. His main interests are in the fields of infectious diseases, particularly tuberculosis; education of health personnel; and health care delivery in different cultural, socioeconomic, and political settings.

Mark S. Thompson received the B.A. from Harvard College and the Ph.D. in public policy from the John F. Kennedy School of Government, Harvard University; he is Assistant to the Director of the International Institute for Applied Systems Analysis in Laxenburg, Austria. He has taught English in Tunisia, and has been employed by the U.S. Department of Health, Education, and Welfare, and by the health care section of the Rand Corporation. Dr. Thompson's research interests include statistics, mathematics, game theory, economics, transportation, and health care systems.